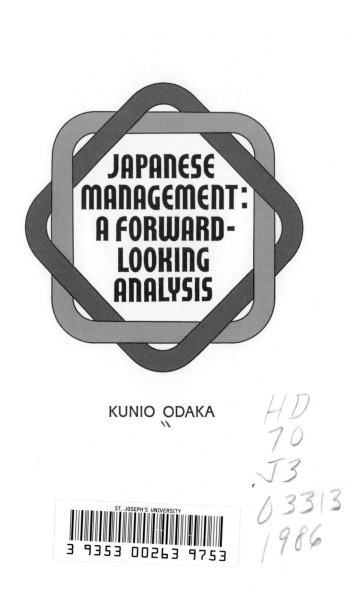

JAPANESE MANAGEMENT: A FORWARD-LOOKING ANALYSIS

KUNIO ODAKA

Tokyo
ASIAN PRODUCTIVITY ORGANIZATION

JAPANESE MANAGEMENT: A FORWARD-LOOKING ANALYSIS

RELEASE

ASIAN PRODUCTIVITY ORGANIZATION

Some other titles published by the Asian Productivity Organization:
- How to Measure Maintenance Performance
- Japan's Quality Control Circles
- Japanese-Style Management: Its Foundations and Prospects
- Management by Objectives: A Japanese Experience
- Modern Production Management: A Japanese Experience
- Organizing for Higher Productivity: An Analysis of Japanese Systems and Practices
- Quality Control Circles at Work
- Guide to Quality Control

Designed and Printed in Hong Kong by

NORDICA INTERNATIONAL LIMITED
for
ASIAN PRODUCTIVITY ORGANIZATION
4-14, Akasaka 8-chome
Minato-ku, Tokyo 107, Japan

© Asian Productivity Organization, 1986

ISBN 92-833-1081-0 (Casebound)
ISBN 92-833-1082-9 (Limpbound)

PREFACE

This is my second book on Japanese management. The first, written shortly after James C. Abegglen's *The Japanese Factory: Aspects of Its Social Organization* came out, was an impassioned rebuttal of Abegglen's assertion that Japanese management is feudal. True, Abegglen had made it clear that he did not regard Japanese management's feudalistic character as a defect. Indeed, he claimed that it was these premodern management traits that enabled Japanese industry to modernize so quickly. It was his thesis that the Japanese management practices which look so old-fashioned to Western eyes — specifically lifelong employment, seniority-based rewards, and the emphasis on harmonious human relations — were eminently compatible with the traditional expectations of Japanese society. According to Abegglen, Japan was successful precisely because it combined these premodern practices with modern production technology imported from the West. Nevertheless, I felt his argument misrepresented and overestimated the principles underlying Japanese management.

My first attempt to correct his thesis was published in a special autumn 1962 issue of the magazine *Bessatsu Chuo Koron*. Later I included this paper in my book *Nihon no Keiei* (Japanese Management, Chuo Koron-sha, 1965). In these writings I was attempting to defend Japanese management.

By the end of 1982, however, my position had undergone a complete reversal. In an article entitled "Nihonteki Keiei no Shinwa to Genjitsu" (The Myth and Reality of Japanese Management) published in the *Nihon Rodo Kyokai Zasshi* (Monthly Journal of the Japan Institute of Labour), besides attempting to correct misimpressions created during the previous decade or so by the foreign myth of Japanese management, I discussed and criticized a number of defects of Japanese management that had recently become impossible to ignore.

This change of viewpoint was not capricious. Over the last twenty years, the myth had escalated and proliferated to create a dangerous situation, especially in Japan. Originally couched in a foreign language, deviating from the reality of Japanese management in several particulars, and tending to praise the good side and ignore the bad, the myth is today finding eager converts among Japanese who use it to justify exaggerated displays of

i

national pride. This situation tends to hide the true nature of Japanese management and to interfere with efforts to correct its by-now conspicuous defects. The ultimate danger is that we may eventually have to scrap the very system of management that has proved so successful.

In addition, the Japanese management boom has spawned much muddled theorizing about the groupistic value orientation on which Japanese management rests. In view of this situation, I have tried in this second book to clarify the concept of groupism and to point out the defects inherent in Japanese management's groupistic practices. The fact that it has these defects, however, does not mean that Japanese management is fatally flawed. To the contrary, this book is also an attempt to propose some specific remedies to revitalize Japanese management and to create a set of Japanese management practices better suited to our modern situation.

While much of the material in this book first appeared in the Monthly Journal of the Japan Institute of Labour, it has been substantially expanded and revised since then. The second half of Chapter 4 and all of Chapters 5 and 6 on groupism and groupistic practices, for example, are completely new.

Kunio Odaka
March 1984

TABLE OF CONTENTS

Chapter 1	**Learning from Japan**	**1**
	Foreign-born Myths	1
	Abegglen's *The Japanese Factory*	2
	Guillain's *Japon, Troisième Grand*	3
	Vogel's *Japan as Number One*	4
	Japan, Inc. and Worker Self-management	5
Chapter 2	**Myth and Reality**	**7**
	The Japanese Management Boom	7
	Myth and Reality	7
	Welcome Salve for Japanese Egos	9
	Echoes of Japanese Fascism	10
Chapter 3	**Japanese Management in the Dual Economic Structure**	**13**
	Is Japanese Management General to All Japanese Enterprises?	13
	No Little Companies Need Apply	16
Chapter 4	**The Source and Development of Japanese Management**	**17**
	The Theory of Immutability vs. The Postwar Evolution Theory	17
	A Third View	19
	The Close-knit Communities of the Edo Period . .	19
	Interpersonal Management and the Close-knit Community	21
	The Source of Japanese Management	23
	Modern Business's Groupistic Management	25
	Is Company Loyalty a Japanese Instinct?	26
Chapter 5	**The Concept of Groupism**	**29**
	Definitions of Groupism	29
	Interpersonalism and Groupism	31
	Paternalistic Management and Groupism	32
	Tribalism and Groupism	33

	Collective Defense and Groupism	34
	Holism and Groupism	35
	Small-Groupism and Groupism	36
Chapter 6	**Groupism as a Cultural Trait**	**39**
	Origins of Groupism	39
	Community Culture in Times of Peace	41
	Does Groupism Transcend Historical Periods? . . .	42
	Groupism as a Cultural Trait	43
	Groupistic Membership and Individualistic Membership	43
	Groupism as the Reason for Japan's Vertical Society	44
	Particularism and Groupism, Universalism and Individualism	45
	Groupism as It Underlies the Culture of Shame . .	46
	Groupism as It Blurs the Line between Public and Private Selves	47
	Groupism as a Cause of *Amae*	48
Chapter 7	**The Advantages of Japanese Management**	**51**
	Advantages and Disadvantages	51
	Employment Stability	52
	Flexible Personnel Policies	53
	Strong Employee Identification with the Company	54
	Changing Perceptions of Japanese Management . .	55
	Japanese Management and Japanese Economic Development	55
Chapter 8	**The Disadvantages of Japanese Management**	**57**
	Four Disadvantages	57
	Encouraging Employee Dependency and Suppressing Individual Creativity	58
	Discriminatory Employment and Impediments to the Formation of a Free Horizontal Labor Market	62
	Harmful Effects of the Escalator System and Middle-management Promotion Gridlock	65
	Work that Gives no Joy and Seemingly Has no Meaning	66
	The Automation Boom and Bureaucratization . . .	67
	Loss of Democratic, Participative Elements	68

	From Joy in Work to Delight in Leisure	69
Chapter 9	**Reforming Japanese Management**	**73**
	Rectifying the Disadvantages	73
	Restructuring Organizations	74
	Meritocratic Personnel Policies	75
	Non-destructive Competition	78
	Less-intrusive Concern for the Employee	78
	Eliminating Employment Discrimination and Encouraging a Horizontal Labor Market	79
	Redesigning the Escalator	80
	Restoring Employee Pride in Work	81
Chapter 10	**Is Japanese Management Transplantable?**	**83**

Chapter 1
LEARNING FROM JAPAN

Foreign-born Myths

The myth of Japanese-style management has spread worldwide. Originating overseas, especially in the United States, this myth has now spread even to the heartland of Japan. It is the collective creation of the many scholars, journalists, and businessmen who were awed at the great prosperity and unparalleled economic growth which Japan achieved so soon after wartime defeat. Although each of these people had his own embellishments, it is the composite of their basic analyses that form the body of what has become known as Japanese-style management.

Japanese-style management as defined in this mythology is the traditional Japanese style of management including lifelong employment, seniority-based hierarchy, employment of the total person, standardized training for all employees, respect for interpersonal harmony, the *ringi* system, *omikoshi* management, collective responsibility, participative management which is at once authoritarian and democratic, and womblike concern for the individual both at work and at home. This Japanese-style management is structured by feudal values which were consolidated in Japanese society as early as the Edo period (1603–1868) but which have been lost in the industrialized West. Nourished by this distinctive social climate, Japanese-style management has been preserved over the ages and now plays a major role as the basis for all personnel and labor management in Japanese organizations large and small — everything from private-sector companies to government offices, schools, and hospitals.

The main impact of Japanese-style management is that the individual employees within the organization are welded together to share a common fate and common goals. The organization assumes responsibility for the total employee, providing him regular training to update job skills, rotating him among jobs to develop well-rounded expertise, and gradually assigning him to positions of greater responsibility as he grows older, such that both the individual and his family feel themselves to be lifelong members of a caring corporate community. Based upon respect for the person, these Japanese-style management practices have been very effective in fostering strong employee loyalty, ensuring labor stability, and creating productive workplaces.

These benefits were already evident when Japan first began to industrialize, and they were a major force enabling Japan to develop faster than any other country in the early years of the twentieth century. Later, after Japan's disastrous defeat in World War II, these strengths came into play again as Japan achieved amazingly rapid economic recovery and enjoyed more than a decade of rapid economic growth beginning in the late 1950s.

Today, management experts from around the world are anxiously studying Japanese-style management to discover the secret of Japanese industry's success in the hope that it will deliver them from the lackluster corporate results in the afterwash of the 1973 oil crisis and halt the erosion of motivation as automation consigns more and more workers to mind-numbing routine.

Abegglen's The Japanese Factory

As early as 1958, the American social scientist James Abegglen and the labor economists Solomon Levine, Frederick Harbison, and Charles Myers had written books embodying the basic materials and outlines of the Japanese management myth.[1] According to Abegglen, the basic personnel practices underlying Japanese management are: lifelong employment (most basic of all); direct recruitment from schools based upon the individual's academic record and character; different recruitment practices for factory and office personnel; rewards and status based not upon performance but upon seniority; collective decision making at the lower levels and the structuring of responsibility; and concern for the employee's welfare which extends even into his personal life.

Japanese-style management brings all of these practices together into an institutional framework designed to make the company, factory, and other artificially structured organizations approximate such naturally evolving associations as the family as closely as possible. This mindset strikes the Western observer as pre-modern or even feudal, yet Abegglen argues that Japanese-style management based upon this feudalistic and illogical mindset was able very early on to take advantage of state-of-the-art Western production technology to astonishing effect, imparting a wondrous vitality to Japanese industry and greatly enhancing Japanese productivity.

---

[1] James C. Abegglen, *The Japanese Factory: Aspects of its Social Organization* (Glencoe, Ill.: Free Press, 1958); Solomon B. Levine, *Industrial Relations in Postwar Japan* (Urbana: University of Illinois Press, 1958); Frederick Harbison and Charles A. Myers, *Management in the Industrial World: An International Analysis* (New York: McGraw-Hill, 1959).

Guillain's Japon, Troisième Grand

Europe also took up this call in the early 1960s as *The Economist* ran a two-part article on Japan which lauded Japan's strong postwar growth and discussed the secrets which had enabled Japanese industry to turn in such a strong performance. This influential thesis ranged even further afield than Abegglen and other Americans in its analysis of the factors and practices which distinguished Japanese-style management.

Japon, Troisième Grand by the French journalist Robert Guillain in 1969 was, like *The Economist*'s articles, a wide-ranging effort to discern the factors which has made it possible for Japan to rise so quickly from the ashes of war to the third-largest economy in the world.[2]

In this book, a best-seller in France, Guillain drew upon his long years of living in Japan to argue that Japan owed its awe-inspiring postwar industrial development to a second industrial revolution sparked by the rapid and widespread introduction of state-of-the-art production equipment from the United States and Europe and to the Japanese worker's near-aberrant devotion to his company and spirit of self-sacrifice, a loyalty which was fostered and maintained by Japan's traditional pattern of industrial relations.

According to Guillain, there are a number of features which characterize industrial relations in Japan. First is the fact that the Japanese employer does not think of the relationship between himself and someone he has employed simply in terms of a labor contract. As seen in the lord-retainer pattern typifying the bulk of relations in Japanese society, the lord (employer) demands unswerving fealty from the retainer (employee) but repays this loyalty by making every effort to ensure that the employee has everything he needs to lead a decent life. At times, the employer will even sacrifice his own wellbeing to provide for his employees, and society at large considers such people exemplary employers.

On the other side of the relationship, the employee sees the company as his primary source of self-identification, and it is the effort to serve the company to the best of his ability which imparts most of the meaning to his life. At the same time, while employees are basically hired hands, they are able to have considerable input in deciding new management policies, initiating new operations, and other actions which would affect them. Thus Japanese industrial relations constitute a vertical society within a more democratic context than is found in the West. Because the employee stays with the same company all his working life, the union representing the employee tends to be an enterprise union or a company union, which further reinforces the employee's loyalty to his company.

---

[2]   Robert Guillain, *Japon, Troisième Grand* (Paris: Editions du Seuil, 1969).

Vogel's Japan as Number One

These studies emphasizing the benefits of Japanese-style management and Japanese-style industrial relations also influenced the 1970 OECD (Organization for Economic Cooperation and Development) report on Japanese labor. After visiting Japan, the OECD study mission concluded that the causes for Japan's rapid economic growth are to be found in Japanese employment's three basic practices of lifelong employment, seniority-based hierarchy, and enterprise unions.[3]

Toward the end of the 1970s, Harvard professor Ezra Vogel wrote his well-known *Japan as Number One* in which, even as he differed with Abegglen and Guillain, he argued that the Japanese company's distinctive organizational structure and management policies are superior and that Americans who hope for continued prosperity would do well to learn from Japan.[4]

In chapter six of this book, which he titled "The Large Company: Identification and Performance", Vogel enumerates a number of distinctively Japanese personnel practices which he says contribute to making Japan number one: lifelong employment; seniority-based hierarchy in determining wages and status; recruitment directly out of schools; limited mid-career employment and restricted employment of older workers; education and training to mold company men who value congeniality over creativity; ceremonies and rituals to foster love of company and a sense of group identification; rotation to ensure broad exposure; downplaying competition and emphasizing cooperation among peers; bottom-up management in which the lower levels do not simply respond to orders from above but take the initiative in drafting and implementing group plans; and a whole host of ways that the company shows it cares about the individual, including family support allowances, retirement pensions, housing loans, company housing, dormitories, gymnasiums and other recreation facilities, social gatherings for the whole family, family-oriented cultural events, year-end parties, parties to bid welcome or farewell to people transferred in or out of a section, festivities to celebrate promotions, and ceremonies to commemorate retirement.

It is precisely because these traditional Japanese management practices have been held over to the present that the Japanese worker still shows unparalleled loyalty and takes pride in contributing to the company's growth by doing his job well. When this Japanese worker mindset combined

---

[3] Ministry of Labor, *OECD Tainichi Rodo Hokokusho* (OECD Report on Japanese Labor, Tokyo: Nihon Rodo Kyokai, 1972).

[4] Ezra F. Vogel, *Japan as Number One: Lessons for America* (Cambridge, Mass.: Harvard University Press, 1979).

with the latest Western production technology, the result was the striking quantitative increases and qualitative enhancement that enabled this impoverished island country to leapfrog into one of the world's leading industrial nations. This astonishing success has often been dissected, but Vogel attributes it not to a mystical group loyalty embedded in the Japanese character but to the fact that Japanese management practices provide workers with a sense of belonging and pride in their work.

Later in the same book, in a section on the American response, Vogel poses the question of whether or not Americans, with their institutions and practices grounded in the value of individualism, can indeed adopt totally alien Japanese management practices, however admirable and effective, and put them to work in American industry without travail and trauma. Basically, Vogel's answer is yes. For all of their significant differences, Vogel says, Japanese and American values and behavioral patterns are surprisingly similar. Both Japan and the United States value the benefits of free competition among companies. America is committed to freedom of speech and freedom of the press, and so is Japan. Japan is generally group-oriented in the sense of placing top priority on the group's survival, but the long history of voluntary associations and the high value attached to teamwork in the United States suggest that group values are not alien to the American way of life. Aside from a few points which might prove intractable, there is no reason America could not adopt the principles of Japanese management for its own.

Japan, Inc. and Worker Self-management

It seems as if there is no end to the formulations of the myth of Japanese-style management. Not long ago, *Newsweek* carried an article entitled "Lessons from Japan, Inc." which maintained that the postwar Japanese economy has been so successful because of Japan, Inc.'s exceedingly close government-business cooperation; the tradition of lifelong employment; and the autonomous small groups such as QC circles in the workplace.[5]

Sensational though the OECD labor report's citing of Japanese management's "three sacred treasures" of lifelong employment, seniority-based hierarchy, and enterprise unions may have been, *Newsweek's* spotlighting of Japan, Inc. and autonomous small group activities in the workplace was downright misleading. Small group activities came to prominence in Japanese industry only in the 1970s, and it is fallacious to link them with the myth of Japanese-style management. This is particularly true of QC circle activities, which were developed spontaneously in a number of large

---

[5]   "Lessons from Japan, Inc.," *Newsweek* (September 8, 1980).

companies to alleviate the disadvantages apparent in traditional Japanese management practices.[6]

It is significant that all of the high priests of the Japanese-management mythology have developed slightly different variations on the same basic theme. Much of the differences in their litanies can be attributed to the different ways different people have reacted to the specter of Japan's awesome postwar industrial development. Yet for all of their differences of emphasis and explanations for the secret of Japanese success, they have interacted with each other to create a durable myth with a wide following among the general public.

---

[6] Kunio Odaka, *Sangyo Shakaigaku Kogi* (Lectures on Industrial Sociology, Tokyo: Iwanami Shoten, 1981): Chapter VIII, pp. 308–315.

Chapter 2
MYTH AND REALITY

The Japanese Management Boom

In the 1980s, this myth spread to give rise to a Japanese management boom not only in the industrialized countries of North America and Western Europe but also in such places as Latin America, Southeast Asia, Korea, and Taiwan. American print and broadcast media have blossomed with frequent specials on the lessons of Japanese management. Seminars on Japanese management draw overflow crowds at American and Canadian universities, and groups of businessmen visit Japan to study Japanese management. America's second-largest automaker, Ford, even renegotiated its contract with the unions to provide for the experimental adoption of lifelong employment and seniority-based wages. In Japan too, the popularity of Japanese-style management theory is having considerable impact.

Myth and Reality

But myth is not reality. Although myths do contain some elements of truth, they are myths precisely because they embroider reality and even, at times, go off completely into the world of fantasy. So is it with the myth of Japanese management. Some of the disparities between the truth of Japanese management and its mythical presentation are:

1. The full list of features characterizing Japanese management is implemented only at large firms and factories, mainly at places staffed by 300 employees or more. The vast majority of Japanese businesses have 10 or fewer employees, and many of these places do not practice any of the features of Japanese management. Such small businesses account for nearly 80% of all companies in manufacturing. Yet the myth would have us believe that these Japanese management practices are widespread at all Japanese firms regardless of size.[1]

2. It may be true that Japanese management has its roots in the Edo period, but Japan has passed through three historical eras in the more than 100 years since then, and Japanese management forms and functions have been modified repeatedly along the way to create the present catechism. A

---

[1] There are exceptions. Vogel, for example, views the practices of Japanese management as being present chiefly in large corporations.

particularly large amount of revamping was done after World War II. The myth, however, would have us believe that Japanese management has continued almost unchanged since being forged out of feudal values.

3. In its concept of such Japanese personnel practices as lifelong employment and seniority-based rewards, the myth is fairly close to reality. In many cases, the terms it uses to describe these practices match long-established Japanese terms. But these labor practices could not have been organized and molded into a distinctly Japanese system of management without some guiding set of values, some model of human relations to approximate. The myth tries to explain this in vague terms with phrases like "similar to a large family", or "the lord-retainer model". One of the authors of the myth even refers to this guiding concept as "the essentially feudal principles of organization".

The term I would suggest for this set of values is "groupism", Although this word is often misinterpreted, it is commonly used in Japan, and I believe it is the best word for the Japanese organization's propensity for putting its priority on the continuity and prosperity of the organization as a whole.

When it comes to the features of Japanese management, however, we need to look closely at these groupistic values to see what they are, when they were internalized in Japanese society, and in what sense they have served as the guiding principle in the formulation of Japanese management's personnel practices. The myth is devoid of such analysis.

4. It is true that Japanese personnel practices do include many of the advantages to the employee that the myth describes, and some of these benefits are extremely important to employees in a Japanese firm, but there are negative aspects as well. In recent years, especially since the recessions of the 1970s, the positive benefits have lost some of their luster and the negative effects have come to the fore. These disadvantages are virtually ignored by the myth.

5. While Japanese management has been a factor in Japan's successful industrial modernization and its outstanding economic growth following World War II, Japanese personnel policies were by no means the only factor in this success story. There were a number of other factors almost completely unrelated to Japanese management practices. It is the cumulative effect of all these factors that accounts for Japan's success. The myth, however, holds that the positive effects of Japanese management – the employment stability, employee loyalty, and the strong sense of corporate self-identity – were mainly responsible.

6. Finally, the myth claims that Japanese management will work well in other countries just as it has worked well in Japan. Although foreign businessmen are certainly free to try to learn all they can from Japanese

management, the disadvantages of Japanese management are coming to outweigh the advantages even in Japan. How can a system which is not even performing as expected at home hope to perform as expected elsewhere? Yet the myth holds that Japanese management is easily transplantable.

This is just a rough list of some of the disparities between the myth and the reality of Japanese management. In later chapters we will consider these features and limitations of Japanese management in more detail. First, however, we must ask why, despite these somewhat obvious discrepancies, Japanese managers, management consultants, economists, and magazine columnists continue to glorify Japanese management as if the whole myth were true.

Welcome Salve for Japanese Egos

Two answers suggest themselves to the question of why Japanese businessmen and scholars so eagerly embrace the myth of Japanese management. The first is simply the attention that has been drawn to this foreign-born myth by its reimportation and sensational repetition over the past decade or so. The primary book that triggered popular interest was Ezra Vogel's *Japan as Number One,* which was translated into Japanese and widely read. Since then, Japanese eyes and ears have been bombarded with information about the myth from sources both foreign and Japanese.

The second answer is that Japanese people subconsciously wanted to believe the myth, or at least wanted to avoid doing anything which would call it into question. It is this second point that I would like to discuss.

The Japanese people have always had a national inferiority complex, a feeling that they lag behind Euro-American countries in many respects. The more intellectual a person is, the stronger this complex tends to be. It has, for example, been pointed out that the Japanese people worry more about their national reputation than any other people because of this subconscious inferiority complex. They are immediately disheartened by foreign criticism, and easily elevated by the slightest foreign praise.

The Japanese reaction to Western praise is the other side of this inferiority complex. Elated at praise, Japanese react uncritically and rarely bother to inquire into the reasons for the praise. Yet Western praise is not always bestowed with complimentary intentions. As some of the sharper commentators have half-seriously suggested, the myth about Japanese management may actually have been a plot to destroy Japanese management and set Japan's industrial development back by puffing Japanese management up with pride, conceit, and complacency.

Triumphant at the praise received, Japanese managers, commentators, and academics have been glorifying the myth and displaying a home-town pride in Japanese management, relentlessly boasting of its good aspects and defending it against all criticism. It is almost futile to confront these people with the negative aspects of Japanese management or to suggest the necessary corrective measures. Instead of trying to understand what is being said to them, they take any criticism as a personal affront and lash back emotionally.

Echoes of Japanese Fascism

Seeing the trend that is occurring in Japan today – the conversion of people to a myth reimported from abroad, and the spread of an attitude of nationalistic glorification and vindication derived from this myth – I cannot help but recall the intellectual climate which prevailed in the years just before World War II when fascism dominated. Then too, farfetched theories about Japan's superiority were rampant, and Japanese traveling abroad made fools of themselves boasting about their country. This is happening again today.

There are several dangers in the recurrence of this type of trend. The first danger is that exaggerated nationalistic pride is psychologically unhealthy, and it can easily be the precursor of intellectual rot.

The second danger is that, if the myth is left unchecked, people may lose sight of the true nature of Japanese management and become unable to evaluate its successes and shortcomings dispassionately.

The third danger is that the school of thought that glorifies Japanese management also tends to deny its defects and hence to disparage any attempts to correct them. The likely result is that the negative aspects of Japanese management will grow unchecked until the whole system has to be scrapped.

These dangers present no great risk to the elite Japanese executives themselves. As long as the Japanese system of management continues to favor management, they are unlikely to see much harm in ignoring its drawbacks for others or allowing these negative aspects to grow unabated. It is Japanese labor, and ultimately the Japanese nation itself, that will suffer if Japanese management is preserved without reform.

Apprehensive about these dangers, I attempted to analyze them and devise ways to rectify the defects of Japanese management in my 1981 book *Sangyo Shakaigaku Kogi* (Lectures on Industrial Sociology).[2] It was not my intention in that book to criticize Japanese management itself or to propose that all of its practices be immediately abandoned. I simply wanted to correct the problems that were becoming increasingly apparent and prevent them from causing untold suffering. Unfortunately, this intention was not well understood. One reason may have been that in

---

[2] Odaka, *Sangyo Shakaigaku Kogi:* Chapter III, pp. 71ff.

attempting to explain the meaning of its subtitle, *A Reform of Japanese Management*, the book overemphasized the negative aspects of Japanese management.

It is in part to avoid such misunderstanding that this present book, besides showing how far divorced the myth of Japanese management is from reality, presents the positive and negative aspects of Japanese management in a more balanced and objective perspective so that the reader himself can see the crying need for reform.

Chapter 3

JAPANESE MANAGEMENT IN THE DUAL ECONOMIC STRUCTURE

Is Japanese Management General to All Japanese Enterprises?

Hearing the term Japanese management, a person is likely to think that it means a style of management unique to Japan and found in Japanese companies of all types and sizes. Unfortunately, he is likely to be wrong. Two points must be borne in mind if this term is to be understood correctly.

The first point is that Japanese management's specific personnel practices are not necessarily unique to Japan. Lifelong employment, for example, is also found in European countries such as West Germany and Switzerland, as are a warm concern for employee welfare and similar practices. What is distinct to Japan is these practices' close integration into a single system of corporate management.

The second, more importnat, point is that, while this systemized set of personnel practices may be unique to Japan, the entire set of seven or eight practices is practiced only in large Japanese industrial corporations: firms or factories with 300 employees or more. It would be a mistake to think that the Japanese management system and its personnel practices are generally used at all Japanese firms and factories regardless of scale. However, surprisingly many people hold this myth-engendered misconception.

It is not unusual for a country to have a small number of large companies coexisting with a large number of small companies, but there are few industrial countries where the differences between the two are as pronounced as in Japan. A mere handful of Japanese workplaces can be considered large, and over 99% have fewer than 300 employees. In the manufacturing sector, only 0.5% of all manufacturing firms had 300 employees or more in 1977, meaning that 99.5% had fewer than 300 employees. Of these small companies, 76.5% had fewer than 10 employees.

There is a pronounced difference in value added per employee and wage levels in the large and the very small sectors. Again looking at manufacturing, the small companies added only 33% as much value and paid their people only 37% as much as the large companies did in 1977. Naturally enough, this vast disparity between the two was due to big business's having more modern production equipment and better technology than small companies had.

Far from being the only difference between very large and very small companies, this difference has also spawned differences in the way they are organized and their personnel policies. The primary difference is that small enterprises are generally much more loosely organized than large ones, but are much more personalized, such that the entire enterprise takes on a community character. In personnel policies also, big business's practices of lifelong employment and seniority-based rewards were never established in many small enterprises, or where they were originally established they became more honored in the breach. There may be a few small enterprises that continue to practice these policies, but they are the exceptions that prove the rule. The reason is not so much that small enterprises cannot afford the full complement of Japanese-style personnel management practices as that there was no need to go to the trouble of formally establishing such a system in small companies.

Evidence that few small companies practice lifelong employment is found in their fairly high annual turnover rate: the rate at which employees leave one company and join another. According to the monthly labor statistics published by the Ministry of Labor, the annual separation rate for 1960 was 33.6% for manufacturers with fewer than 300 employees, while it was only 18.6% for large manufacturing firms with 500 employees or more. Of course, even the large companies' 18.6% is not very low. Before and immediately after the war, the separation rate of regular male employees at large firms was frequently only a few percent, but since the war the fabled lifelong employment system has become increasingly unable to hold employees at large companies.

According to a survey Abegglen conducted for his book on the Japanese factory, the annual separation rate for regular male employees during the five-year postwar period from 1949 through 1953 was only 2.5% at one major electrical equipment manufacturer in Osaka. Even at the company with the highest sepration rate, a Shikoku textile plant, the rate was only 3.6% for male employees in the five-year period from 1951 through 1955. With figures like these, it is not hard to infer that most regular workers who were not forced to quit their jobs for health or other personal reasons remained with the same firm until they reached retirement age, and it was from such data that Abegglen argued that lifelong employment was a basic personnel policy at Japanese corporations. The corporations that Abegglen surveyed, however, were all large concerns with 3,000 employees or more.

Things are different at Japan's small companies. Even before World War II, the annual separation rate at small firms was much higher than what

Abegglen found. After the war, it commonly ran 30% or more in the decade of rapid economic growth in the 1960s. While it did decline somewhat during the recession of the 1970s, in 1969, on the eve of that decade, manufacturing firms with 30 to 99 employees recorded a separation rate of 31.2%. In other words, of every 100 people who worked for these firms at the beginning of 1969, over 30 had departed to work elsewhere by the end of the year.

Although this is not as high a separation rate as in the United States, it is certainly no lower than for the industrialized countries of Western Europe during the same period. If Japanese workers at small firms were no more likely to spend their entire careers with one company than industrial workers in Western Europe, that means that the practice of lifelong employment at the small Japanese firms where they worked was not strong enough to keep them from going elsewhere.

While it is difficult to find equally convincing data concerning the system of seniority-based rewards, three facts suggest that most smaller Japanese firms never had such a system: (1) the high separation rate that has existed among workers at small firms, as seen above; (2) the shorter employment records typical of people at small firms; and (3) the major wage disparities for middle-aged and older employees at large and small firms, even though entry-level younger employees are paid comparable wages at all companies. Had small Japanese companies practiced seniority-based wages, their employee separation rate should have been lower, their employment records should have stayed with them longer, and the salaries they paid should have gone up with age and years of service.

One reason advanced to explain the lack of seniority-based rewards at these small firms is that they also lack a strong labor movement, since it was the enterprise unions that argued the need to preserve the life-pattern, seniority-based wage schedules at the large Japanese firms in the early postwar years. Yet regardless of the reason, it is clear that the small companies have not instituted seniority-based rewards.

Given that the small company was basically a community in itself, there was no great need for it to adopt such other Japanese-style personnel practices as standardized education and training, the emphasis on interpersonal harmony, the *ringi* system of having people sign on to bottom-up proposals, *omikoshi* management in which everybody carries the company but no one person seems to dominate, and personal concern for each employee's welfare. Rather, it was the large corporations, which had always been more like aggregations of individuals brought together by the profit motive and which were forced to enlarge and rationalize their organizations and centralize and dehumanize their management as time went on, that needed to resort to artificial, planned policies to create the community atmosphere that was inherent to the small company.

No Little Companies Need Apply

It should be clear why the nearly 80% of Japanese firms with fewer than 10 employees do not practice the Japanese management espoused by the myth, and why only very few of the 99% of manufacturing firms with fewer than 300 employees have instituted the total package of Japanese management practices. Even at large corporations famed for practicing lifelong employment and seniority-based rewards, these practices apply only to regular, full-time employees, and it would be unusual indeed for them to be applied to any of the many temporary employees, day laborers, part-time workers, and other non-permanent personnel that these firms hire.

By describing the Japanese-style management practices as if they applied to all workers at all Japanese firms, the myth presents a very misleading picture of reality.

Chapter 4

THE SOURCE AND DEVELOPMENT OF JAPANESE MANAGEMENT

The Theory of Immutability vs. The Postwar Evolution Theory

According to the popular myth, Japanese management developed in its prototype form during the Edo period and has been preserved intact through the vicissitudes of subsequent ages down to the present day. This interpretation, however, represents only one of two opposing theories as to when Japanese management first developed and how it evolved. In reality Japanese management has changed and evolved throughout its long history, and did not reach its present form until after World War II.

We shall call the first of the two opposing views the theory of immutability. Like the myth, it holds that Japanese management developed in the distant past of the Edo period and has endured to the present day nearly unchanged. Supporters of this first view, the theory of immutability, include Abegglen and Levine, who provided much of the early evidence for the myth. According to these people, the original practices of Japanese management developed almost spontaneously in the feudal period before the Meiji Restoration of 1868 and have been preserved and skillfully managed from then on through the postwar period. In this sense, Japanese management practices are holdovers from the feudal period.[1]

By contrast, the second view holds that Japanese management practices were frequently modified, and that their present form was born of necessity in the aftermath of World War II. This second view we shall call the postwar evolution theory.

The postwar evolution theory rejects the idea that Japanese management is a holdover from the feudal period and its premodern value sets. Rather, this theory holds that Japanese management practices were artificially developed later, mostly after World War II, out of the need to compete successfully in domestic and foreign markets and in response to the persistent demands of labor unions. The ultimate reason for their

---

[1]   Abegglen, *The Japanese Factory:* pp. 130–135; Levine, *Industrial Relations in Postwar Japan:* pp. 18, 32–35.

introduction at large Japanese companies was to satisfy and retain employees by giving the company a type of community character, a character that was rapidly being lost in the years after the war. This same policy need was also seen in Western countries with more advanced production facilities and technology. In that sense, the newly developed Japanese management practices, far from being feudal, were indicative of the advanced state of Japanese industry.

This theory of postwar evolution has much to recommend it. This is clear, for example, in the way in which lifelong employment and the seniority-based rewards system, two of the key practices of Japanese management, have been strengthened and reaffirmed in this century, especially since the war.

Japanese enterprises were already practicing long-term employment for their white-collar employees before World War I, but this did not extend to blue-collar workers. After that war, in the 1920s, Japanese companies, finding themselves faced with a severe shortage of skilled labor, began showing greater concern for the total person, providing regular training, and otherwise working to retain employee loyalty and services permanently. This was the start of real lifetime employment for these people.

Given further impetus by legislation restricting labor mobility during World War II, lifetime employment was preserved after the war by the labor unions' fight for job stability. The history of these events was detailed in my *Nihon no Keiei* (Japanese Management) published in 1965.[2]

The seniority-based wage system did not finally become established in large Japanese corporations until after World War II. Most of these corporations had previously paid wages on personalized schedules that emphasized age, academic record, and years of service. Thus their efforts to adopt the Western practice of paying wages according to position and ability were opposed by the enterprise unions organized at most large firms after the war. The unions argued that personalized, seniority-based wages answered labor's needs better and was a more acceptable wage standard. These union demands forced Japanese managers to reaffirm seniority-based wages and rewards in large Japanese companies.

The postwar evolution theory thus holds that some of the most prominent practices of Japanese management, far from being holdovers from the feudal age, are the result of deliberate policies instituted after World War II. In no sense are they reincarnations of any prototype form of Japanese management based on premodern values.

Many of the proponents of the postwar evolution theory hold that, since modern Japanese management practices were developed in response to

---

[2] Kunio Odaka, *Nihon no Keiei* (Tokyo: Chuo Koron-sha, 1965): pp. 18–19.

needs that arose during the postwar period's rapid industrialization and growing domestic and international competition, they are quite capable of being transplanted to other modern industrial countries. Professor Masumi Tsuda of Hitotsubashi University, for example, has asserted this view for some time,[3] and he has recently been joined by a number of foreign commentators.

A Third View

Although it may seem strange for there to be two drastically conflicting theories about when a given set of personnel policies was established, such disagreement is by no means unusual. What we have here are two theories each stubbornly affirming one side of the same set of facts while denying the other completely.

As so often happens in such cases, the truth is somewhere in between, i.e.: The original form of Japanese management was, as the theory of immutability argues, molded out of values underlying Japanese society during the Edo period. In this prototype form, including both positive and negative aspects, it endured over the years until the end of World War II. Yet as the postwar evolution theory contends, Japanese management was modified and strengthened over the long decades of Japanese industrialization in the late nineteenth and early twentieth centuries, and it did not emerge in its present form until after World War II.

Any discussions of Japanese management today must deal with Japanese personnel practices in their present form. However, even though this present form has undergone substantial evolution, it must be recognized that Japanese management still retains its original character and effectiveness. The forces that produced the Japanese management prototype, for all its strengths and weaknesses, are still with us today.

The Close-knit Communities of the Edo Period

Given this historical development of Japanese management, the next question is how it originally arose. In attempting to answer this question, we must first look at the seventeenth and eighteenth century society and the various close-knit communities that sprang up throughout Japan during that period.

The shogunate that Tokugawa Ieyasu founded in Edo in 1603 divided Japan into a large number of fiefs created by consolidating the domains the *daimyo* lords had held since the late sixteenth century. Each fief included the villages that already existed within its realm and the families that had

---

[3] Masumi Tsuda, *Nihonteki Keiei no Yogo* (Vindicating Japanese Management, Tokyo: Toyo Keizai Shinpo-sha, 1976).

settled in them.

The word family here does not mean the nuclear family consisting of a husband and wife and their children, but the patriarchal extended family banded together to pursue wet-paddy rice farming in the traditional manner. A village of such families was a natural unit, unlike the artificial administrative units of modern times. Like the village families, the village itself was primarily engaged in growing rice in irrigated paddies. Given the demands of this work, the village's families and individuals had to cooperate to perform this work as efficiently as possible, and their cooperation readily extended to their other daily activities which they undertook to ensure the entire village's continuity and prosperity.

To the people who lived in them, these families and villages were close-knit communities sharing a common fate: each a community of people bound by kinship, land, or other natural ties, living together permanently in one place as a self-sufficient group in the true spirit of harmony and cooperation. The reason for calling such a community close-knit is that its members were completely immersed in it for their whole lives. Once a person become a member of such a community, regardless of his role and accomplishments, he was inseparable from the community and its destiny.

While the family and the village units arose spontaneously, the fiefs were artificially established for military or political reasons. Yet since the society and social structures which they encompassed consisted of a number of family and village communities, so in time did the fiefs themselves come to take on many of the features of these close-knit communities. During the 265 years that the Tokugawa shogunate lasted, many such close-knit communities were formed and flourished throughout Japan. There were several factors that made this possible.

The first factor was that the main occupation of the members of these communities was, as we have seen above, wet paddy farming. It was neither commerce nor industry, occupations that keep people constantly moving to different places, but agriculture — the tilling of paddies by generation after generation of people living permanently in the same place. Having this land-rooted occupation basic to their entire way of life facilitated the formation of close-knit communities.

Perhaps even more important, however, were the special political and societal conditions of the Edo period. The Tokugawa shogunate brought peace to the land after nearly 150 years of civil war. When Tokugawa Ieyasu united the country under a stable, orderly government, the resulting political situation naturally favored the formation and prosperity of all sorts of close-knit communities, large and small. This was further encouraged by the shogunate's policy of sealing out foreign influence as the Tokugawa shogunate protected these close-knit communities from being undermined by foreign culture and civilization. Christianity, for example, was an important factor in fostering individualism in the West but remained inconsequential in Japan during these centuries.

Interpersonal Management and the Close-knit Community

The close-knit communities that developed under the Tokugawa shogunate operated on the basis of a number of personal management principles or, from the standpoint of the community members, behavioral norms:

1. Total, lifelong membership. Most of the members of the close-knit community were born and raised in it, worked in it, lived in it, and belonged to it totally from childhood on. Typically, they spent their entire lives within the community. If events forced them to go into the outside world, they carried their community status and duties with them, and retained these permanently. Throughout their lives, their destinies as individuals were tied up with the destiny of their community.

2. The duty of selfless devotion to the community. The primary duty of a member of a close-knit community was to devote himself selflessly to the continued well-being of the community as a whole. There must have been people in these communities who desired personal distinction and happiness, but such desires were suppressed as the sustained, patient effort to ensure the continuity, prosperity, peace, and happiness of the group took precedence. Not until these things had been achieved for the community as a whole could individual members benefit from them, in proportion to the effort each had put into their attainment.

3. Discipline and seniority-based rank. Whether born or adopted into a household that already belonged to the village community; the individual's status in the community was defined from the very beginning as that of his household. From a young age, formally recognized members of the community were taught discipline and correct behavior so that they could grow into capable community leaders. They were taught not only the rules of personal relationships but also rules of moderation in food and dress and the accepted uses of leisure time. They also received thorough training in the household occupation, so that they could contribute properly to it, and through it to the life of the community. Although the training varied slightly from community to community, it was usually fixed and uniform in each community, aimed at turning out well-integrated community members. Little attention was paid to developing the individual's personality, talents, or ambitions. In fact this type of education was avoided because it might produce heretics who would disrupt the community order.

Young people brought up under this discipline were first set to easy tasks as apprentices or helpers. As they grew older and gained experience, they were given more difficult and important work. As their roles changed, so did their status and the treatment accorded them. Thus arose the system of seniority distinctions among community members, and the seniority-based hierarchy.

4. Harmony and concerted efforts. A single close-knit community often contained subcommunities within it, either present from the beginning or created subsequent to the community's formation. In every village there were, for example, the separate constituent families, groupings of clan and kinship, and age groupings. Within a family, the subgroupings might include the main family and several branch families, direct and collateral bloodlines, and the group of hired hands. Each grouping would have its own role and rank, but the different groups were always expected to cooperate with each other and to respect the hierarchy of their relative positions. For its own continuity and well-being, the community demanded that its subcommunities work together to create and preserve harmony for concerted community efforts.

It was also important to maintain and promote harmony within the subcommunities. Harmony within the subcommunity may even have been more important, because without it there could not be true cooperation among the different subcommunities. One of the basic beliefs of the community leaders was that harmony among the members of the subcommunities was a motivating factor for all community members. It was to promote harmony within the group that competition among the members of a subcommunity was suppressed, attempts to gain advantage over other people were quashed, and equivalent rank and treatment were accorded to group members of the same age cohort.

Because of these practices of harmony and concerted effort, less capable members who were unable to perform their set tasks well and delinquent members who abandoned their duties were helped out by the rest of their subcommunity and were gradually socialized to fit in with the group. After a while, they came to have the pride and feeling of worth that accrued from contributing to the entire community.

5. Authoritarian management and participative management. The highest status among the members of a close-knit community belonged to the village headman, the heads of households and other elders, and the leading adults appointed as their assistants. Having the authority to speak on behalf of the entire community's interests and needs, these people demanded absolute obedience from the general community at large.

In running the community's affairs, however, these men of authority did not use the arbitrary, one-sided decision-making process of despot kings or autocratic company presidents. In principle, all important decisions concerning the ruling and running of the community were made in councils, with all members participating. The elders' duty was to pass final judgement on the results reached by the council.

Decisions in the various subgroups generated within the close-knit community were made in basically the same way, with the participation of all members. The oft-cited *ringi* system is simply the institutionalization of this type of decision-making process. What Vogel called the Japanese "bottom-up" method of corporate management already existed in the close-knit communities of the Edo period.

This Japanese management was participative in the sense that all members of the group joined in deciding its directions and planning its activities. Participation was a major feature of these close-knit communities. The reverse side of participation's coin — that no member of the group was individually responsible or even had to feel responsible for whether the policies and plans everyone decided on succeeded or failed — was equally important. Responsibility for the group's decisions and their implementations was borne not by individual members but by the group as a whole.

6. Concern for the person's total welfare. The final important feature of these close-knit communities was the way they looked after their members, seeing that they had the necessities of life: food, shelter, and clothing; protection and safety; education and training; health and hygiene; and leisure and entertainment. The peace and happiness of the life of the group could not be achieved without satisfying its members' needs.

If the community had not shown such concern for the welfare of its members, they would probably not have been willing, no matter how closely their own fate was linked with the group's, to give it their continued devotion and service. But with the members belonging to the group with their whole beings for their whole lives, it was natural for the close-knit community to show a constant, warm concern for the total life of each member. At the same time, however, the close-knit community's all-embracing concern for its members' well-being sometimes had the undesired effect of spoiling them and making them overly dependent on the community.

The Source of Japanese Management

The principles of personal management in these close-knit communities furnished their members with behavioral norms and structured their shared existence. By following these behavioral norms in their continuing common life, they were able to make their close-knit community a place of happiness, comfort, and peace. Satisfied with their community life, they could take pride in the worth of their daily work and devote themselves to the preservation and prosperity of the group.

This was no mean achievement. In later years, when more modern organizations were created in Japan's urban centers, the founders and managers of those organizations had the wit to try to make them as much like the former close-knit communities as possible. It was no accident that they modeled their personnel practices on the principles of personal management generally found in the close-knit communities. The value set that guided this wisdom was the theory that we are calling "groupism".

However, this theory was first applied to create imitations of the close-knit communities long before corporations, factories, trading companies, and the like began to appear in Japan's cities. The commercial application of the values of groupism – the embryo forms of the Japanese management pattern – actually took place around the middle of the Edo period. The artificial bodies to which groupism was applied were still too small to be called "modern organization"; they lacked modern facilities, and their management was not very "rationalized". They were the mercantile houses with shops in large cities.

In the beginning of the eighteenth century, for example, the Mitsui, Konoike, Sumitomo, and other large mercantile houses flourished in Osaka, Kyoto, and Edo. These mercantile houses were originally family businesses, but they also engaged in shipping, mining, pharmacy, money-changing, money-lending, and other activities. They were quite distinct from the original close-knit communities, which were located in the country and practiced agriculture as their main occupation, but this very distance was all the more reason for their founders and managers to consciously model their shops and other places of business upon the former close-knit communities. The fact that their personnel practices were based upon the principles of personal management originally found in the close-knit communities was one of the secrets of their success.

Proof that such modeling actually took place can be found in the family precepts of these mercantile houses. According to Professor Yotaro Sakudo, a management historian at Osaka University, the major practices of later-day Japanese management, including lifelong employment, the seniority-based hierarchy, the apprentice system, training and discipline, respect for harmony, group decision-making, and humanistic management, were often emphasized in the family precepts of the mercantile houses of Osaka and vicinity as basic precepts for employee management. Systematic Japanese management practices based on the theory of groupism already existed in a primitive but visible form in the eighteenth century.[4]

The fact that this special set of practices was inscribed in the family precepts is indicative of how effective they were in the mercantile houses' management. Indeed, large mercantile houses practicing this early form of

---

[4] Yotaro Sakudo, *Showa-Kyoho no Keiei* (Management in the Showa-Kyoho Period, Tokyo: Diamondo-sha, 1978): Chapter I.

Japanese management were established not only in the three large cities of Osaka, Kyoto, and Edo but also in outlying castle towns as well. During the long period between its original formation and the end of World War II, however, Japanese management was frequently modified to satisfy evolving requirements. According to Professor Sakudo, these modifications had already begun in the Edo period. Further modifications were made in the late nineteenth and early twentieth centuries, when Japan's industrial modernization was beginning to "take off" and modern enterprises were springing up all over the country. The pace of changes was particularly evident at the larger enterprises as they rationalized their organizations to make better use of the new, power-driven facilities they were installing.

Modern Business's Groupistic Management

The groupistic management that was applied in Japan's new, urban firms and factories around the turn of the twentieth century had the same ultimate objectives as the groupistic theory applied by the Osaka mercantile families in the eighteenth century but was adopted for slightly different reasons. In eighteenth century feudal Japan, groupism was applied to organizations that had started as close-knit communities but had become so large that they were losing their original community character, and groupistic management was intended to revive this community character and group values.

In the firms and factories of the late nineteenth and early twentieth centuries, groupism was applied to organizations that had never been close-knit communities but were completely new creations, rationally and artificially constructed in imitation of the corporate organizations of the advanced industrial countries of the West. Thus groupism was instituted and institutionalized at these organizations in order to make them more like the close-knit communities of old and, by introducing groupistic management practices modeled on the communities' personal management, to instill them with a community spirit and vigor.

Japanese management is not a style of corporate management that developed spontaneously at any one point in time or any one firm. Rather, the system of Japanese management practices was created intentionally and systematically to make the new corporate organizations resemble the successful close-knit communities of the past despite their modernity, rationality, and artificiality. Not created at any one particular time by any one individual or individuals, it was molded over a long period, undergoing modification and development at the hands of many individuals. What remained constant throughout the process of its formation was the effort to make the modern, artificial corporation a vital entity by imbuing employees with the spirit of company loyalty, community identification, and pride in their work.

Is Company Loyalty a Japanese Instinct?

Although the modern Japanese company as it emerged in the late nineteenth century was an artificial creation patterned after Western models, it was not simply an organization created for a single purpose. It was also a *gesellschaft* – a company of individuals gathered together for their mutual benefit. No matter how culturally homogeneous the Japanese people might be, no matter how infused they might be with the spirit of harmony and cooperation, the new organizations were ultimately comprised of people, both labor and management, pursuing their own individual interests. The bigger the enterprises grew and the more the individual's role was compartmentalized, mechanized, and automated, the truer this became. If the employees of such a *gesellschaft* had been left to work simply for the corporate profit, without receiving any independence or autonomy, they would eventually have lost their will to work for and identification with the company. They would have become the type of employees who are quick to gripe where their own ambitions and desires are concerned but are completely indifferent to the company's needs and interests.

Only the uninformed outsider, or nationalist seeking something to extol in the Japanese character, could believe that all Japanese have some kind of innate loyalty that would prevent the disintegration of the company even if nothing were done to strengthen and consolidate personal relations. Even if it could be demonstrated that modern Japanese workers are more loyal to their companies than American or West German workers, this would probably have to be done with a survey conducted at a Japanese company that had been practicing groupistic management and fostering employee loyalty for some time. Loyalty to the company is by no means an innate or instinctive Japanese trait.

Today as in the past, Japanese who work for a company work for their own needs and interests. If they work willingly, it is because the work satisfies their own needs and does not involve any undue suffering or sacrifice. If forced to perform dull, repetitive, compartmentalized tasks in a mechanized or automated plant without any discretionary freedom, even the most diligent Japanese worker will eventually lose the will to work and fail to identify with the company.

In fact, this very trend was already evident among employees at large, impersonal companies in the earlier-industrializing countries. Starting in the late nineteenth century, the enterpreneurs and managers of modern Japanese firms realized that Japan would suffer the same problem of labor alienation, with all of its dangerous consequences for their companies' survival and growth, if they allowed their companies to remain mere associations in the *gesellschaft* sense.

One option open to them for preventing such alienation was to take advantage of the employee's own self-interest to tie him to the company with rationalized working conditions, efficiency pay, and improved treatment. This policy left the *gesellschaft* character of the corporation unchanged. The other side of this policy was to sharply limit the employee's actions and to punish or fire lazy or disobedient workers. This was the usual policy in the industrialized Western countries, and it was adopted by many of Japan's early modern companies.

Yet as the disadvantages of this policy orientation became evident starting in the early years of the twentieth century, large Japanese corporations shifted their personnel practices to the second option of conceiving the modern company's artificial structure as analogous to the close-knit communities of an earlier time. In effect, this was an effort to introduce groupistic management practices modeled on the personal management principles of the close-knit communities and hence to suppress the *gesellschaft* aspects and highlight the communal *gemeinschaft* aspects. On the whole, this policy was successful. Companies that introduced groupistic management practices found they had heightened the spirit of harmony, cooperation, and employee loyalty, people took pride in their work and its social worth, and there tended to be less personnel turnover. Because of these positive results and despite the serious problems inherent within the system, these groupistic management practices were preserved through World War II to become institutionalized at large corporations as fodder for the Japanese management myth.

Chapter 5
THE CONCEPT OF GROUPISM

Definitions of Groupism

The distinctively Japanese system of personnel practices known as Japanese management was thus born of groupistic values applied to modern enterprises and organizations. Because, however, the terms groupistic and groupism have been frequently misunderstood and misused, it is necessary here to take a more detailed look at the concept of groupism and the analogous concepts of interpersonalism, paternalistic management, tribalism, holism, and small-groupism.

A simple definition of groupism can be found in my *Sangyo Shakaigaku Kogi,* where I defined it as a "value orientation" in which a group or organization, in this case usually a corporation, "perceives itself as a close-knit community with a shared destiny" and therefore "places less emphasis on realizing its members' potential and satisfying their individual aspirations than on ensuring continued well-being of the whole and the overall peace and happiness of the group".[1] This definition itself has received enough discussion that no further comment is needed here, but some explanation may be in order of three of the expressions used in it: (1) "perceives itself as a close-knit community with a shared destiny", (2) "places less emphasis on realizing its members' potential", and (3) "value orientation".

Concerning the first, "perceives itself as a close-knit community with a shared destiny", it should be understood that, since the function of the group is to assure its members' peace and happiness, groupism was necessarily modeled on the families, villages, and fiefs that flourished in the Edo period. As a result, the group's personnel practices were modeled on the principles of personal management that had been so successful in those close-knit communities.

The groups to which the concept of groupism was applied, however, were modern organizations and other artificial bodies that either had never been close-knit communities or, like the mercantile houses of Osaka and environs, had once been a type of close-knit community but had lost most of their community character. The phrase "perceives itself as a close-knit

---

[1]   Odaka, *Sangyo Shakaigaku Kogi:* Chapter II, pp. 43-46.

community with a shared destiny" thus implies a group that is not itself a naturally evolving close-knit community but that chooses to adopt management practices imitative of the close-knit communities' principles of personal management in order to approximate these communities as closely as possible.

Concerning "places less emphasis on realizing its members' potential", it should be recalled that the primary principle of the close-knit communities was the overriding importance which they place on the continued well-being of the whole and the overall peace and happiness of the total community. This concept of the whole's taking priority over the individual was naturally included when modern organizations adopted the groupistic value orientation in an attempt to create management practices modeled on the behavioral norms of the close-knit communities. As a result, the modern organization stressed the continued well-being, peace, and happiness of the whole group, and placed "less emphasis on realizing its members' potential and satisfying their individual aspirations".

This does not, however, mean that the individual's personality, special talents, and aspirations were completely suppressed or ignored in groupistic management practices. The inclination of groupistic management practices was to allow individuals to express their native capabilities but to grind out the rough edges in the individual's personality, talents, and aspirations to make them compatible with the functioning of the organization. In other words, the aim of Japanese management is to create large numbers of people who are very competent but are not prima donnas and then to weld these people together in the company's interests. The management policy of restraining undue competition among employees and maintaining harmony in line with the old Japanese saw about "hammering down the nail that sticks up" should be understood in this light.

Lest it be misunderstood, it should be pointed out that the "members' potential" here refers not to the employee's ability to perform the work required by the organization, his work experience, or his resulting work record or seniority, but to the innate talents that the person is born with, his creative sense, skills or habits learned before joining the organization, and his earlier-formed dreams and aspirations that he continues to hold after joining the organization. In saying that the individual is ground down, I do not mean that the individual's ability to do the work or the results he achieved were ignored, but rather that his capabilities, creativity, and long-standing aspirations as an individual were ignored.

Concerning "value orientation", what does it mean to say that groupism is a value orientation? In sociological behavioral theory, value orientation is used to mean: When a person given a choice among different objectives and among different means of obtaining them engages in a given behavior, he always tries to select the objectives or means that have the higher value, and this attitude toward the selection is his value orientation. As such, the term is synonymous with value set. It is a theory, or way of thought, that directs a person to select or emulate things of higher value.

The groupistic value orientation was an attitude that recognized the close-knit communities as groups with higher-value structures and functions and tried to pattern the groups or organizations on them as closely as possible. Following this value orientation, the founders and managers of the modern enterprises that sprang up during Japan's industrial take-off tried to institute a system of personnel practices modeled on the close-knit communities' principles of personal management, and in this way what we know today as Japanese management was gradually created.

There is some question, of course, about whether or not the word "groupism" is appropriate to describe the basic value orientation underlying Japanese management policies. This word is a direct translation of the Japanese term *shudan-shugi* (*shudan* meaning group and *shugi* meaning -ism), but it is not a word commonly used in ordinary English. An alternative term would be "group-centered pattern of value orientations", but even this alternative does not resolve the confusion because "group-centered" may carry connotations of the group as a self-righteous, transcendental, and restrictive group exercising dictatorial control over its members, whereas the actual group in the Japanese organization is a harmonious, close-knit community or *gemeinschaft* within which the individual members can satisfy most of their own life needs. Accordingly, working for the continued well-being of such a close-knit community was actually the best way for members of the group to provide for their individual happiness and satisfy their own needs. That is the theory meant by a "group-centered" value orientation.

This said, groupism may perhaps best be understood in comparison with a number of analogous concepts.

Interpersonalism and Groupism

Professor Eshun Hamaguchi of the Faculty of Human Sciences of Osaka University has recently suggested that the basic premise of Japanese management should be called interpersonalism.[2] Hamaguchi's point is that the structuring principle of all Japanese groups and organizations, corporations included, is not a group-oriented value set that submerges the in-individual in a supra-personal, restrictive totality that suppresses the

---

[2]   Eshun Hamaguchi, *Kanjin-shugi no Shakai Nihon* (Japan as a Society of Inter-personalism, Tokyo: Toyo Keizai Shinpo-sha, 1982).

individual and self-assertion suppressed for the good of the whole but an interpersonal value set that attempts to form a harmonious, "common-good, common-life" social system with its members' behavior considerate of other people's needs.

Hamaguchi's proposal, which is reminiscent of the concept of society asserted by Tetsuro Watsuji in his *Ningen no Gaku toshite no Rinrigaku* (Ethics as a Science of Interpersonal Relations, Iwanami Zensho, 1934) is an interesting and certainly significant argument. Unfortunately, it rests on a confusion of the concept of groupism with the concept of holism. The group referred to in the term "groupism" is not a totalitarian group submerging the individual in a self-righteous, transcendental whole wantonly ignoring individual needs and self-assertion for the good of the whole. Rather, as noted above, it is a *gemeinschaft* ruled by harmony and coexistence, satisfying nearly all of its members' life needs, and permitting a degree of spontaneous participation in the making of important decisions affecting the management of the group. With this as the meaning of the word group in "groupism", there is no need to resort to the alternative term (interpersonalism) proposed by Hamaguchi and nothing is achieved with such a substitution.

Paternalistic Management and Groupism

The concept of paternalistic management has frequently been invoked in discussions of the principles underlying Japanese management. Although this term is not an artificially coined term such as interpersonalism and does not deviate substantially from the concept of groupism as described above, there are still two major reasons for not adopting it.

Paternalistic management resembles groupism in being a value orientation that aims to provide newly created modern organizations with a system of management modeled on the close-knit community and its behavioral norms. To call this value orientation "paternalistic management", however, is to suggest that its aims are confined to behavior, thoughts, and modes modeled on the life and hierarchy of a family or other kinship community. The aims of groupism extend further — to behavioral modes and thought patterns modeled on the life of communities held together by geographical, political, and military non-kinship bonds.

The second reason for avoiding the term "paternalistic management" is that it risks laying undue stress on management's concern for the paternalistic and *gemeinschaft*-type personal relationships. These elements are only part of the practices of groupism. The groupistic value orientation's ideal is not a simplistic *gemeinschaft* in which people join in altruistic and unselfish friendship, helping each other, forgiving each other, encouraging each other, and sparing no efforts on each other's behalf. In the actual close-knit communities of old, there were rigid relationships of authority and obedience, as between master and servant, relationships of envy and rivalry between fellows and brethren, and open contention among members over such things as irrigation water rights. There were also severe sanctions and punishments for those who violated these structural rules, including ostracism, torture, and crucifixion. There were not infrequent skirmishes and haggling among group members for personal gain, such as are regularly seen in business. The close-knit communities were a *gemeinschaft* that embraced these actions and confrontations and provided a framework that blunted their bite. By contrast, the concept of paternalistic management excludes most of these elements and projects the image of a pure, cultivated *gemeinschaft*.

Tribalism and Groupism

According to one school of thought, it is a distinctive trait of Japanese to form a visible, tangible group by collecting and dwelling in the same place when any significant number of them share a common life or common work. The members of the group belong to it totally, and cooperate in their work or for the group's continued well-being.

Human groups are created in two basic ways: A group of people sharing a similar outlook may live gregariously in one place to form a tangible group, in which case it is prerequisite for the formation of the group that a large number of people be collected together in one place; or separate individuals may make a pact of mutual cooperation based on a shared purpose, ideology, or qualification, forming an intangible (symbolic) group, in which case the existence of individuals with the same purpose, ideology, or qualification is prerequisite to the group's formation. In all situations, the Japanese tendency is toward the first type of group formation, and this school of thought holds that this Japanese trait, or value orientation, to prefer groups with large numbers of people living together gregariously in one place amounts to tribalism.

Leading spokesmen for this school include Professor Gregory Clark, a former journalist and British diplomat before becoming an academic at Sophia University, and *Tate Shakai no Ningen Kankei* (Human Relations in a Vertical Society) author Chie Nakane, professor at the University of Tokyo. In his recent book *The Japanese Tribe: Origins of a Nation's Uniqueness,* Clark argues that Japanese society is an anachronism that did not lose its ancient tribal character until quite recently, for which reason the Japanese people have been able to maintain their groupistic value orientation up to the present.[3] Working from this premise, Clark makes

---

[3] Gregory Clark, *The Japanese Tribe: Origins of a Nation's Uniqueness* (Tokyo: Simul Press, 1977).

a number of very interesting observations about modern Japanese behavior. Yet what Clark is referring to is not so much groupism as tribalism, as shown by the fact that the true aim of groupism is not so much to have a large number of people live in one place, which is what Clark is talking about, as to bring the group as close together as possible as a close-knit community.

More generally, the term "groupism" as used in this text does not mean people who, sharing common purposes, interests, or views, are adverse to acting independently or in individual styles and who, given the opportunity, will form a group to help each other in the pursuit of their shared purposes or interests. While some Japanese do exhibit that propensity or value orientation to a striking degree, it is not what I mean by the term "groupism".

Collective Defense and Groupism

Another, similar interpretation of groupism is that it is a type of "collective defense". This interpretation points out that the Japanese natural environment has always been a harsh one of storms, earthquakes, and other natural disasters, and that the Japanese people have generally been so poor as to make self-sufficiency difficult. Thus it was largely to protect themselves from these hazards that they formed firm communal groups and developed a pattern of helping each other, depending on each other, and working for harmony and the common good. It is these groups and their behavioral patterns which have given rise to the groupistic value orientation.

In other words, these communal groups were collective defense organizations created to protect people against poverty and the elements. The practices necessary for collective defense, including total identification with the group, authoritative control by elders, the stress on harmony and concerted efforts, and the group's concern for the members' whole livelihood, arose nearly spontaneously. Later, when modern enterprises spread throughout Japan, this tradition was followed and the communal practices necessary for collective defense were instituted in these enterprises, these practices withstanding the vicissitudes of time to be preserved until the very present as, according to this interpretation's advocates, Japanese management.

This interpretation can be found in the writings of Professor Nagamasa Ito, author of the headline-getting *Shudan-shugi no Saihakken* (Rediscovering Groupism), and Professor Hiroshi Hazama, author of *Nihonteki Keiei – Shudan-shugi no Kozai* (The Groupistic Structure of Japanese

Management).[4] These two authors' works are important writings that directly confront the issue of the relation between Japanese management and groupism, and much can be learned from them. I cannot, however, agree with Ito's attributing the birth of groupism to the harsh environmental conditions that Japanese face daily or with Hazama's attributing it to Japanese poverty and the "international crisis mentality". The Japanese are not the only people that have dwelled in poverty in a land fraught with natural dangers. Many of the peoples of Southeast Asia's underdeveloped countries or the Middle East's desert lands live in greater poverty and more precarious conditions than the Japanese, yet these people's social life is not necessarily characterized by the groupistic value orientation and customs. In regions where Islam, Christianity, or other universal religions are strong, it is even possible to find individualistic social thought patterns and behavioral standards. The theory that Japanese groupism originally arose as a collective defense mechanism to protect people from natural disasters and poverty is thus difficult to substantiate.

In addition, if groupism is simply a value orientation for collective defense, as Ito and Hazama claim, why was this value orientation adopted for the formation of modern Japan's industrial take-off when these organizations consisted of people who were in no particular danger from either the forces of nature or the threat of poverty? It is difficult to see how corporate groupism can be adequately explained as a collective defense mechanism.

Holism and Groupism

There are also writers who, while using the term "groupism", confuse it with the concept of holism. This is not surprising; many people find the two terms easy to confuse in that groupism is primarily an anti-individualistic concept for group generation and holism is one of the main anti-individualistic group-generating principles.

The essential difference between the two terms lies in the different meanings they attach to the common concept of "placing a higher priority on the needs of the whole than on the needs of the individual". While the groupistic concept encompasses the idea that the prosperity and happiness of the group should be emphasized over the personalities and individual needs of its members, this does not mean that satisfaction of the group's needs is a categorical imperative for which individual personality and self-assertion can be completely suppressed and sacrificed. If the priority of the whole is interpreted that way, the group becomes an entity transcending its

---

[4] Nagamasa Ito, *Shudan-shugi no Saihakken* (Tokyo: Diamondo-sha, 1969); Hiroshi Hazama, *Nihonteki Keiei − Shudan-shugi no Kozai* (Tokyo: Nikkei Shinsho, 1971).

individual members and having its own needs and objectives completely divorced from its members' needs and objectives. As a self-righteous, transcendental whole, it attempts to use its members as mere tools to satisfy its own requirements and achieve its own objectives. The "whole" hopes that its "tools" will be diligent and perform well, but it does not regard diligence and good performance as voluntary contributions toward the whole's objectives. Rather, it employs constant restriction, supervision, and coercion to ensure that each member's work and performance is useful to the whole.

The group in groupism is not such a self-righteous, transcendental whole, and it could even be argued that the ultimate purpose of the group's prosperity and happiness is to enhance its members' well-being. In the groupistic concept of the priority of the whole, the benefits accruing to the individual members are premised upon but not exclusive of prosperity and happiness's being achieved for the whole group. In the process of achieving prosperity and happiness for the whole, groupism does not completely suppress or sacrifice its members' individuality or right to self-assertion. Rather, it expects each individual to employ his individuality and special skills voluntarily as best he can.

Groupism differs from individualism, however, in not permitting individual efforts to achieve the group's needs and objectives to be exercised in individualism's *laissez-faire* way. In groupism, the individual's intentions and efforts are controlled and limited so that they will contribute to achieving the objectives of the whole in an accepted way. It is in this sense that the individual is "ground down" and socialized.

The difference between the groupistic value orientation and the holistic value orientation should thus be clear: While holism is concerned only with the priority of the whole, groupism respects both the priority of the whole and the freedom and happiness of the individual.

Small-Groupism and Groupism

One final misinterpretation of the term "groupism" has arisen from the small-group activities (QC circles and the like) that spread in Japanese workplaces in the 1970s, as some observers have argued that these small-group activities are based on the same groupistic theory that underlies Japanese management practices.

When small-group activities were discussed as one of the three Japanese management practices in the *Newsweek* article "Lessons from Japan, Inc.", for example, they were depicted as having arisen from the groupistic value set. Yet as already noted above, this is a distortion of both Japanese management practices and their underlying groupistic value set. These autonomous small-group activities, which have recently become so popular in Japanese workplaces, are actually not the product of groupism at all. Rather, they are based on new ideas introduced to remedy some of the disadvantages that time has made increasingly apparent in Japan's groupistic management practices)

As already explained, the system of Japanese management practices contained certain participative or autonomous management practices, expressed by the terms *omikoshi* management, consensus management, and bottom-up management. So long as these practices were functioning, Japanese management's organizational structure of centralized authority and oppressive restrictions was considerably alleviated and a measure of individual freedom permitted.

With the rapid automation after World War II, however, these traditional participative management practices gradually came to be more form than substance and lost their leavening quality. At the same time, the rigid, authoritarian, bureaucratic character that had always been present in Japanese management organizations came to the fore. As a result, the rank and file at these organizations began to take less interest in their work and the quality of their products began to decline. It was to counter this deteriorative trend that, starting around 1970, small-group activities were started among the rank-and-file workers at large Japanese manufacturing firms.[5]

Once the origin of these small-group activities is understood, it becomes apparent that their underlying value orientation — "small-groupism" as it has been called — is completely different from the groupistic value orientation that gave rise to the traditional system of Japanese management.

A better term for the practice in which workers spontaneously form small groups or teams to manage their own work would be the "small-group system" or "teamwork system". This system has been used not just in Japan but throughout the world. Employees in the Western industrial countries, for example, willingly adopted this system when the work was particularly difficult or required collective creativity.

Completely unrelated to the groups in the term "groupism", these small groups generally consist of about ten people with special skills for doing a certain type of work who talk together, make suggestions to each other, and more or less spontaneously form a group which will spontaneously disband when the work is completed. While this type of small group of people who have banded together to perform a given task has a definite shape as long as the task continues, its members remain essentially separate individuals. They have merely formed a temporary alliance to achieve a common objective, and the value orientation underlying these small-group activities is actually closer to individualism than to groupism.

---

[5] Odaka, *Sangyo Shakaigaku Kogi*: Chapter VIII.

Chapter 6
GROUPISM AS A CULTURAL TRAIT

Origins of Groupism

As already seen, Abegglen and Levine, two of the founders of the myth of Japanese management, speak of the equivalent of groupism. Although they do not use the term groupism per se, they do speak of the feudal group-generating principles that predated Japan's industrial modernization. Their point in this characterization was that these principles created a system of Japanese management practices that, when combined with modern production technology from the industrialized West, led to astonishing advances in productivity. This is an interesting point, but their use of the word "feudal" with its implications that groupism is a holdover from the feudal age and that the Japanese mindset is somehow backward or retarded is difficult to accept.

The value orientation that I call groupism did not arise as part of the authoritarian social system of Japan's feudal period, nor was it expressly a concept of that period alone. Given the right set of conditions, groupism was capable of arising before the feudal period, and once it became established it was capable of outlasting the times in which it arose. Rather than being the product of any particular age, the groupistic value orientation is a Japanese cultural trait.

If the origins of groupism are traced back, they will be found in an early form that came into existence in the social life of the Japanese people in the Edo period, when the country was closed to the outside world and controlled by a feudalistic system. Most of the life of that period took place in rural communities consisting of large numbers of families living in one place and engaging in wet paddy farming as their main occupation. Had the main occupation been hunting or livestock raising, as it was in the West, they would not have come together in permanent villages with families residing in one place for generation after generation, the village would not have evolved as a close-knit community with a shared destiny, and the groupistic value orientation would not have been formed.

But in fact, most of the villages that evolved naturally in Japan in this period did grow into close-knit communities, as did their individual families. Living gregariously in these close-knit communities, people were able to live totally as life-long community members, entrusting their fates to the community, devoting their entire lives to their occupations, and thereby achieving prosperity and happiness for themselves and their families.

The idea of the priority of the whole arose naturally in these close-knit communities, and the community members naturally followed it. The whole that had the priority to them, however, was the particular, closed, close-knit community to which they belonged, and this priority of the whole in no way meant that the peace and welfare of society at large took priority over all else. Had Japanese society been under the influence of a universal, monotheistic religion such as Christianity, and had its behavioral norms been based on the individual's own conscience, the particularistic notion of the priority of the whole within the close-knit community might not have taken hold, at least not in the same form, but it did.

Within these close-knit communities, around the concept of the priority of the whole there naturally grew up the behavioral principles and customs described earlier: discipline and training, seniority-based hierarchy, authoritarian control, participative management, joint responsibility, respect for harmony, and warm concern for all aspects of an individual's life. Within the resulting stability, people were able to devote themselves to their work and to maintain the patient, sustained efforts that achieved their own and their families' happiness and prosperity.

Life was by no means easy in Edo-period Japan, and famine and natural disaster brought dire misfortune upon the people from time to time. In addition, life was made even harder if the head of the fief was despotic or misguided. Nevertheless, village life during that period was on the whole stable, and, inwardly at least, the people lived in a personal fullness and harmony made possible chiefly by the distinctive customs and behavioral rules of the close-knit community born of their own native wisdom.

The close-knit village communities of the Edo period may not have been utopias, but they set the standard of communal life for most of the people at the time. The attitude that the village framework of community life was the standard against which other life patterns were to be measured was the start of the value orientation that I call groupism.

Needless to say, the people of Edo-period Japan did not "perceive themselves as close-knit communities" or "perceive themselves as analogous to close-knit communities". They did not have to; they *were* close-knit communities. It was only later, when the actual close-knit communities had largely disappeared, that analogies to them were perceived and the idea arose that the new, modern organizations should be created to approximate the old, true close-knit communities as closely as possible, with behavioral norms within the organization modeled on the close-knit community's principles of personal management. This was the start of the value orientation described by the term groupism.

Community Culture in Times of Peace

The groupistic value orientation was not the product of a particular age but could have arisen in any age under the right conditions, and, once established, it could easily outlast the period in which it arose. Thus groupism is not an expression of Japanese feudalism, as Abegglen and Levine suggest, but is a Japanese cultural trait.

Lest there be any misunderstanding, it may be in order here to explain this in more detail. One of the "right conditions" for the appearance of groupism is that peace prevail throughout the land. A second condition is that during this time of peace, society must consist basically of village communities engaged primarily in wet paddy farming. These are the two main conditions. Other conditions, such as the absence of a strong and disruptive universal religion such as Christianity, could be cited, but these can be disregarded here.

During the Edo period, peace held sway for more than two and a half centuries under the shogunate's policies of feudal government and national isolation. This era amply satisfied our two conditions. Groupism could just as easily have arisen in other ages, such as the Heian period, when these two conditions were also satisfied; and conversely, it could not have arisen in the Heian period, the Edo period, or any other period had these two conditions not been satisfied. Groupism was actually one part of the village community culture that appeared in times of peace like the Edo period.

There have been times in Japanese history during which the exact opposite of groupism prevailed, ages of struggle when Japan was ruled by the law of the jungle. The period of the Northern and Southern Courts (fourteenth century) and the period of Warring States (fifteenth and sixteenth centuries) were two such ages. During these periods, the major groupistic principles of personal management – harmony, cooperation, and concern for others – were rarely to be seen, and would have been generally ridiculed if they had been expressed. The prevailing ideas of those ages were competition, spoils to the victor, and all is fair in love and war. These were dog-eat-dog times. The relationship between master and servant was respected, but there was little sense of loyalty to any group. Individualism was the prevailing value orientation.

This combative, individualistic value orientation has also been evident in more recent times: in the political chaos that followed the Meiji Restoration of 1868, for example, and even more recently in the postwar period of rapid economic growth. In these more recent cases, however, the movement did not go very far, and was only temporary. In time, political and economic stability were restored and the harmonious groupistic value set again became dominant. A historical relationship can thus be discerned between the political and economic climate of an age and the waxing or waning of the groupistic value set.

Assuming this interpretation is correct, the groupistic value set that characterizes Japanese culture must have gone through repeated cycles of dominance and recessiveness from the distant past to the present. Groupism is not the only world view that has appeared in Japanese history. As just seen, there has been at least one other world view: one diametrically opposed to groupism. These two world views – groupism and individualism – have competed with each other throughout history. Both have been present in every age, but one or the other side of the coin of the Japanese personality prevailed to become the dominant world view in any given age. Which of the two prevailed was determined by the political and economic climate of the age, and by whether it was a time of peace or an era of tumult.

Yet although the pendulum swung back and forth, neither of the two world views ever completely eclipsed the other or eradicated it, as has happened in Western history. Throughout Japanese history, both world views existed, either separate or in combination.

Does Groupism Transcend Historical Periods?

The second point concerning the historical character of groupism is closely related to the first. Once groupism became established it outlasted the period in which it arose, but not indefinitely. Like any other value set or cultural trait, it came and went.

Groupism was part of the village community culture that flourished in the peace of the Edo period. Far from being an expression of Japanese backwardness, it was a Japanese cultural trait that arose in a certain period and was able to influence society for several generations beyond the end of that period.

With the breakup of the naturally formed villages and the shift from the patriarchal family toward the nuclear family, however, the village community culture gradually declined and groupism's validity as a group-generating principle was gradually eroded. Even so, when modern Japanese industry was in its take-off period in the late nineteenth and early twentieth centuries, more than 65% of the Japanese population still lived in rural villages, so that there were still many people who had personally experienced the quality of village community life and culture, or had been told of it by parents or grandparents. Shortly after World War II, however, rural villages accounted for less than half of Japan's population, and twenty years after that (in 1970) the figure had dropped to 18%. Moreover, the rural villages in which this declining fraction of the population lived were no longer naturally formed villages but were artificially drawn jurisdictions, the natural villages having been erased by the rapid land reforms and village consolidations of the postwar period.

By the time Japan started its rapid postwar economic growth, few of the people knew the importance of village community culture or understood the significance of the attempt to apply the groupistic value set to modern organizations. In many cases, it was simple inertia that led to the adoption of these groupistic principles in organizations during the postwar period of rapid economic growth.

Groupism as a Cultural Trait

In this discussion of the origins of groupism, I have frequently referred to groupism as a Japanese cultural trait. In support of this assertion, it is in order here to examine six instances in which groupism, despite having lost some of its force, remains one of the basic value orientations governing Japanese society: groupistic membership and individualistic membership, groupism as the reason for Japan's vertical society, particularism and groupism, groupism as it underlies the culture of shame, groupism as it blurs the line between public and private selves, and groupism as a cause of *amae*.

Groupistic Membership and Individualistic Membership

It has always been true that Japanese joining a group tend to join it totally if it is important to them. The person no longer thinks of himself simply as an individual but instead identifies with the group. Rather than being a lone individual, the collegian is "a Waseda man" and the businessman "a Matsushita man". For both the individual and others, the person's self-image is the group's image. This group identification comes from the Japanese tendency to regard the groups they belong to, or belonged to for any length of time, as close-knit communities.

Today, most close-knit communities have disappeared and their place has been taken by modern groups that are artificial organizations created for specific purposes. Because these are narrow-purpose groups, a person may easily belong to several groups at once. However, the groupistic tendency to identify with them completely and behave accordingly remains.

In modern Western society, a person belonging to several groups at the same time usually gives only part of himself to each of them. Groups like the modern family, school, corporation, labor union, church, and political party were created for separate purposes, and a person belonging to several groups at once belongs to each only with that part of himself that corresponds to the need the group is able to fulfill. If these groups are thought of as circles and the individual as a smaller circle, the smaller circle of the self is not located completely within any of the larger group circles. Its center remains outside all of the group circles. This mode of group belonging is what is meant by "individualistic membership".

A Japanese, however, belongs to each of the groups with his whole person. The circle representing the self lies completely within the larger circles of family, school, company, labor union, and political party. These group circles overlap, of course, but no matter how much they overlap, the individual's self circle still remains inside them. This mode of group belonging may be called groupistic membership.

The persistent prevelence of groupistic membership in Japan has given rise to some special customs rarely seen in Western Europe or North America. For example, it is still common to treat chance seniority relationships arising in the school or workplace with the same deference as the older-younger fraternal relationships in the patriarchal family or the hierarchical relationships that dominated rural village life. In another example, people who have been thrown together by chance as classmates for three or four years hold regular alumni meetings at which, notwithstanding their occupational differences, their different social statuses, and their different lifestyles, they still address each other with the casualness of bosom friends who have grown up together in a close-knit community. These customs are arguably unique to Japan.

Groupism as the Reason for Japan's Vertical Society

As a result of their tendency to groupistic membership, Japanese tend to regard rank and hierarchy in the modern organization as symbolic of the individual's worth. Whereas Western civilization regards rank and status within, say, a corporation or government office as valid only within that organization, the Japanese, because he belongs to the organization in the groupistic sense, tends to think of these relationships as valid for the whole person in all of life: as implying rank or status in the human race. One's superior at the company or government office is not just one's superior at work but is regarded as a superior sort of person, a cut above the rest even outside of the work context. Even in non-work situations, people who are subordinate at work generally defer toward their superior and put themselves generally at his service. For example, if the boss is moving, people feel compelled to help out even though this has nothing to do with their official duties at work. If the boss's house catches fire, they feel compelled to rush to the scene and help put the fire out. All of this comes from the Japanese tendency to regard rank within the organization as implying status within the human race.

It was Professor Chie Nakane who popularized the view that Japanese society is a vertical society in which personal relationships within the group are mainly vertical.[1] Yet whereas Nakane claimed that these vertical human relationships came from a traditional Japanese over-sensitivity to rank within groups, I would say that they come from the Japanese tendency toward total-person groupistic membership. When a person belongs to a group totally, the vertical relationships within the group tend, in Japan, to extend beyond the group and are regarded as signifying people's vertical relationships as human beings.

Particularism and Groupism, Universalism and Individualism

The American sociologist Talcott Parsons classified value orientations into a number of patterns depending upon the values the individual ("the actor") regards as important standards by which to evaluate societal conditions and human interactions and to determine what actions are appropriate.[2] Depicted in diagrammatic form, these value orientations appear as "pattern variables" including several dichotomies, such as particularism and universalism, or achievement and ascription. Particularism is the value orientation that stresses the significance of special situations involving the actor himself; and universalism the opposite value orientation in that it is not concerned with particular relationships but stresses universally existent relationships of general validity. The achievement-ascription dichotomy concerns one actor's evaluation of another: whether he stresses the results or status the other person has attained through his own talents and efforts (achievement) or the other person's innate attributes and inherited status (ascription).

How do these patterns apply to the groupistic value orientation? In adhering to groupism, the Japanese are generally particularists in that the close-knit family, village, and fief communities, as well as the modern organizations perceived as analogous to them, had a limited membership and were closed wholes serving their members alone. These closed communities are thus unlike the open and universalist society implied in such expressions as "the citizenry", "modern society", "the international community", and "the human race". Unlike these open and universalist societies, the closed group has a specific life of its own independent of the role and status of its members.

Groupism is, above all else, a value orientation in which people belong totally to a particular, individual whole and devote their lives to the welfare and prosperity of the whole. Duty, devotion, and responsibility toward the

---

[1] Chie Nakane, *Tate Shakai no Ningen Kankei* (Human Relations in a Vertical Society, Tokyo: Kodansha Gendai Shinsho, 1967).

[2] Talcott Parsons and Edward Shils, eds., *Toward a General Theory of Action* (Cambridge, Mass.: Harvard University Press, 1951): pp. 76-88.

openly universal society do not count for much in the groupistic value orientation. What are important are duty, devotion, and responsibility toward the particular, closed group.

Japanese religious beliefs have also been groupistic and hence particularistic. The indigenous Japanese Shinto religion was not a universal religion worshiping one absolute God, like Christianity and Islam, but basically an ancestor worship placing its faith in the specific protective gods of the family, village, or country. Even after universalistic Buddhism's acceptance in Japanese society, belief in these specific gods continued and Buddhism was amalgamated with native beliefs such that its universal deity was accepted as just another of the traditional specific gods, albeit a special one. Similarly, the Japanese attitude toward work, tempered by the belief in these specific gods, is different from the Western attitude of devotion to duty nurtured by a belief in the virtue of glorifying an absolute God. In that the Japanese believes that the way to achieve oneness with the specific group's protective god is to devote oneself to the peace and order of the particular close-knit community to which one belongs, even if it is actually a modern organization only patterned after the close-knit community, the well-known Japanese diligence is primarily a groupistic diligence.

While Japanese particularism appears at first blush to be akin to the ascriptive evaluative norm in Parsons' pattern scheme, Robert Bellah, a disciple of Parsons's, argues that the dominant value system in traditional Japanese social life was one conjoining particularism with achievement. By contrast, he says, the basic American value orientation is a combination of achievement and universalism and the guiding values in Chinese social life are those of ascription and particularism.[3]

Interesting though Bellah's observation is, and while it may be true that the Japanese value system is characterized by the combination of particularism and achievement, the dominant Chinese value system would seem to me to be a combination of ascription and universalism, not particularism. How else are we to explain the fact that Japanese-type groupism has not been a major tendency in Chinese history?

Groupism as It Underlies the Culture of Shame

In her book *The Chrysanthemum and the Sword,* the American social anthropologist Ruth Benedict described Japanese culture as a culture of shame totally different from the Western culture of guilt.[4] According to

---

3   Robert N. Bellah, *Tokugawa Religion: The Values of Pre-Industrial Japan* (Glencoe, Ill.: Free Press, 1957): Chapter II.

4   Ruth Benedict, *The Chrysanthemum and the Sword: Patterns of Japanese Culture* (Boston: Houghton Mifflin, 1946): pp. 222-224.

Benedict, the primary punishment a person suffers for his sins against God in the Euro-American value set is the torment of his own conscience, and this can only be relieved by confession and atonement. In the Japanese value set, however, the worst punishment a person can suffer is to be shamed and ridiculed by one's special circle of acquaintances. Shame cannot be relieved by confession. Conversely, if there is no public shame involved, the Japanese need have no fear, no matter what sins he might commit.

Benedict's characterization of Japanese culture is also a clue to understanding Japanese groupism and particularism. To a Western brought up under Christianity, the paramount imperative is to fulfill his responsibilities and to act correctly toward the open, universalistic society controlled by an absolute God. The Western idea of correct behavior is constructed on a value orientation that unites universalism with individualism by requiring the individual to obey universal dictates. Within this value orientation, sins are punished by the individual's torment of conscience at having violated a universal dictate.

For the Japanese, however, having been brought up in a culture in which devotion and duty toward the welfare and prosperity of the particular, closed group to which he belongs is paramount, correct behavior means obedience to the special dictates of the particular group and misconduct is therefore punished by rebuke, shame, or humiliation before the group. To be shamed by the group that the person belongs to is an extremely harsh punishment, and one not easily lived down so long as he remains a member of the group. However, as Benedict points out, misconduct that does not evoke the group's scorn is punishment-free.

Groupism as It Blurs the Line between Public and Private Selves

If, as Benedict says, Japanese culture is a culture of shame, the shame-based Japanese morality is basically an other-directed morality in which the major sanction is what others think of one. To take this idea to its extreme, in a society governed by this type of morality, nothing is wrong, no matter how heinous, so long as it does not shame the doer in others' eyes.

It goes without saying that actions that earn praise and gratitude within a particular group are not necessarily praiseworthy within the larger society. Nevertheless, it is typical of other-directed morality that the ultimate standard against which an action is judged is whether or not it will win praise and gratitude within the individual's particular, closed group.

Given Japan's long exposure to other cultures, one would expect the idea of civic duty and public morality to have seeped into the Japanese consciousness, but there are still people who fail to see the distinction between their public and private selves. Such a person might, for example, break a national law to benefit his own political cronies, and so long as this misdeed is appreciated by his faction or cronies, he sees nothing wrong with flouting the public weal to flaunt his private zeal. Groupism is largely to blame for this situation.

Groupism as a Cause of Amae

In his best-selling book *Amae no Kozo* (*The Anatomy of Dependence*), Professor Takeo Doi of the National Institute of Mental Health argued that the passive demand for love expressed by the Japanese word *amae* is the key to understanding the Japanese personality structure. This psychological state is common among infants in other countries, but only in Japan does the person continue to angle for favoritism even after he becomes an adult.[5] Although he is a psychiatrist by training, Doi bases his argument on data derived from comparative linguistics rather than from psychoanalytic methods. According to Doi, neither English nor German has a word corresponding to the Japanese *amae*, whereas Japanese has numerous ways to express this sentiment: *tayoru* (depend on), *nedaru* (coax or tease), *nareru* (take for granted), and *namete kakaru* (treat as a pushover) among others. The *amae* sentiment is one of always secretly expecting protection, favors, and considerate concern from other people as a natural right; and of feeling betrayed if these expectations are not met, in which case *amae* turns into alienation, sulking, and resentment. In short, *amae* is a complex psychological tendency involving a feeling of powerlessness deriving from the lack of an independent spirit, and a dependency on what one considers one's natural entitlement of protection and special favors.

Why is this psychological tendency so prevalent in Japan? Doi provides many clues, but he does not arrive at any definitive answer. Might not this Japanese *amae* come from the groupistic value orientation? As seen above, groupism entails perceiving the group or organization to which one belongs as analogous to the close-knit community of the rural village of old and modeling the organization's practices and behavioral norms as closely as possible on those of the close-knit community. Until the breakup of the close-knit communities that followed the end of World War II, groupism was the heart of middle-Japan, and even today it remains the basic value orientation for people who were born and raised in rural communities.

To these people, the close-knit communities that they identified with from childhood were *gemeinschafts* from which they could naturally expect to receive protection, special favors, and considerate concern. Although the corporations and government bureaucracies that they identify with now are

---

[5]   Takeo Doi, *Amae no Kozo* (Tokyo: Kobundo, 1971).

not actually close-knit communities, groupism's adherents feel that these modern organizations should accord them the same kind of *amae* as their close-knit communities did. Groupism is thus one major reason why *amae* is so widespread in Japan.

Chapter 7
THE ADVANTAGES OF JAPANESE MANAGEMENT

Advantages and Disadvantages

The traditional Japanese system of corporate management is characterized by:

Lifelong employment

Employment of the total person

Standardized training to ensure that everyone is of average competence

Job rotation to produce generalists

Seniority-based rewards (rank, salary, and perks)

Aversion to competition and emphasis on harmony

The *ringi* system

Omikoshi management and group responsibility

Organization at once authoritative and democratically participative

Compassionate concern for employees, including their personal lives

An embryo form of this managerial system was already discernible in the large mercantile houses of eighteenth-century Osaka and environs. As these firms grew into modern enterprises, there was a conscious attempt to apply this system in the giant organization. This Japanese experiment with traditional management practices, first as a natural evolution and later as a conscious culture-creation, has succeeded in meeting most of its objectives.

There have, however, been certain negative effects which, at first only latent, have become serious enough since the late 1960s to raise questions about the efficacy of Japanese management. The Japanese management myth says almost nothing about these disadvantages. This may be because the disadvantages had not yet become very apparent when the myth was first taking shape. Or it may be that the disadvantages were apparent but the creators of the myth failed to notice them. Or perhaps they noticed them but chose to ignore them. At any rate, the myth emphasizes only the advantages of Japanese management.

This is typical of myths in general, since the whole purpose of a myth is to lend credibility to and sanctify an object or practice. Unchallenged, however, the Japanese management myth could cause the Japanese people not only to lose sight of the truth about Japanese management but even to fall prey to dangerous illusions of racial superiority. It is thus necessary in this discussion of Japanese management to deal with its disadvantages as well as its advantages, to ask what the causes and probable consequences of these disadvantages are, and to seek ways to rectify the shortcomings without sacrificing the advantages. Yet before discussing these disadvantages, it is perhaps appropriate to take another look at the advantages that actually accrue from Japanese management, to separate them from the hype that is in the myth, and to examine their workings.

Although many advantages have been cited for Japanese management as it has evolved over the years, the three most important seem to be:

1. Employment stability
2. Flexible personnel policies
3. Strong employee identification with the company

Employment Stability

Three factors contribute to employment stability. First, once an employee is hired by a company, as long as he does what he is told, co-operates with his co-workers, and does a passably good job, his employment is generally secure even if his record is not particularly outstanding. Short of some extreme crisis, he does not have to worry about losing his job. As he attains seniority, he can expect to be promoted to increasingly important positions and to benefit from the warm protection and personalized attention of the corporation until the day he retires.

Second, the company supplies its regular employees with everything they need to do their work. The new employee who has been hired for life under the Japanese management system will find that the company selects his job for him; decides where he will work; supplies him with the necessary clothing, tools, machinery, equipment, and materials; provides him with companionship; gives him detailed instructions and training; and pays him a regular salary with benefits just to do his job as he is told, when he is told, and where he is told. Nor is that all. The company also has extensive welfare facilities and services for its employees, including dormitories and low-cost family housing. The company both hires and looks after the total person.

Third, Japanese management is structured to ensure a congenial atmosphere in the workplace. This goes further than simply stressing the importance of maintaining harmony. Efforts are also made to eliminate anything that might disrupt the interpersonal harmony. For example, people working together are matched as closely as possible in age and qualifications. In work-skill training, ability disparities resulting from people's innate talents are ground down so that all the employees in a given workplace are as nearly equal as possible. If someone still tries to disrupt things by showing off his individual abilities, he is penalized with social disapproval and other means of "hammering down the nail that sticks out." In addition, the practice of determining salary not by the subjective standards of personnel ratings or performance evaluations but by the objectively impersonal standard of age and years of service contributes to congeniality by eliminating a major cause of envy and resentment among workers. Because they are not competing, employees are able to work together in the true spirit of concerted effort, helping each other, sharing their knowledge without reservation, and relying upon one another.

Employment stability is particularly attractive to young people newly joining a company, especially those born and raised in close-knit rural communities. For such people seeking urban employment − as for urban youths educated in postwar democracy − work stability is equivalent to a second home.

This employment stability, including lifelong employment, employment of the total person, seniority-based rewards, and respect for human harmony, is a major factor inevitably giving rise to the advantage of enhanced employee loyalty to the company.

One word of caution is in order, however. Employment stability is an advantage only for the ordinary, obedient young person lacking in individuality or ambition, the typical employee of old Japan. To the increasing number of young people with individualistic ideas, employment stability can be seen as confining and restrictive.

Flexible Personnel Policies

Flexible personnel policies are also attributable to three factors. For one, in choosing new employees, the company does not look for people who already have specific experience and skills. Rather, it chooses people for their character, upbringing, and family background, employs them as total people, gives them standardized training to teach them average competence in the skills the company needs, rotates them from job to job to give them well-rounded experience, and draws upon the capabilities employees acquire as they move toward retirement.

Within this, personnel are exposed from an early stage to as many different types of work as possible, so that no matter where they are later placed, no matter what work they are assigned, they will be able to adapt. The aim is to create versatile employees. The advantages of this practice become strikingly obvious when automation leaves the company with large numbers of excess personnel who must be transferred to other jobs. Because of their broad experience and adaptability, employees suddenly assigned to new jobs can adapt to their new work and new co-workers relatively quickly. Japanese management's flexible personnel policies are thus policies creating readily adaptable personnel.

Closely related to this is the flexible use of personnel. The "internal labor market" frequently remarked on by foreign observers is a distinctive Japanese feature deriving from lifelong employment and a seniority-based hierarchy. A Japanese firm with a well-developed internal labor market has the option of quickly transferring a person who is unqualified for a certain kind of work or is not doing well in a given workplace to another kind of work or workplace where his new assignment will make better use of his capabilities. Under this system, no worker anywhere need be considered in-the-way, incompetent, or incapable. Transferred to a new workplace, workers can develop a sense of self-esteem which will encourage them to work harder and do better.

Among the distinctively Japanese practices underlying personnel flexibility are those of lifelong employment, standardized training, job rotation, and seniority-based rewards; and the advantages of personnel flexibility are closely related to employment stability in that they enable employees to devote themselves to the company's work for their entire careers. For the company too, flexibility is highly effective in making best use of each employee's capabilities regardless of their short-term performance.

It should also be pointed out, however, that personnel flexibility is applied only within the context of the corporation and can actually be detrimental in that it tends to produce workers who are custom-tailored to the company where they work and useless anywhere else.

Strong Employee Identification with the Company

The third advantage of Japanese management results from the preceding two advantages plus certain other factors. Strong identification with the company means that the employee identifies with the company to such an extent that he regards his career and his fate as inseparable from the destiny of the company. This feeling is nurtured and reinforced by employment stability and personnel flexibility, as well as by the respect for harmony, participative *omikoshi* management, and the company's considerate concern for the employee's total welfare.

Employees who identify with their company naturally have a strong sense of company loyalty and are highly motivated, but such company loyalty is extremely difficult to instill. Yet despite this difficulty, Japanese management has routinely been instilling strong company-identification among employees for years. Little wonder that foreign managers envy the Japanese company's seemingly easy success in developing employee loyalty, good morale, and strong motivation and want to learn from Japanese management practices.

Once again, however, a word of caution is necessary. The good morale that derives from a strong identification with the company is different from the good morale that derives from taking pride and joy in one's work. Morale and motivation that depend on identification with the company can easily evaporate if people are tied down day after day to dull, repetitive, and mind-numbing jobs. Adherents of Japanese management tend to overlook the complex interactions of all of these many factors in generating employee identification and other managerial advantages.

Changing Perceptions of Japanese Management

All of the above advantages of Japanese management deserve the high esteem they have won, yet the drawbacks in Japanese management have become increasingly apparent since the end of World War II, and Japanese management has lost some of its luster as a growing number of people no longer consider it an unmixed blessing. Many people no longer see Japanese management's advantages as advantages. Such negative thinking has been especially pronounced during and after Japan's era of rapid economic growth as increasing numbers of young people have evinced a preference for individuality and a strong desire to test their own powers. Within the company these are the people most likely to form their own teams to carry out their own projects their own way, as free as possible from corporate restrictions. People like these are unlikely to view stable employment and flexible personnel management as advantages pure and simple. As the number of such people increases, the number who fit the company-man mold and who identify strongly with their company is on the decrease.

The advantages of Japanese management thus have less appeal today than in the past, and they are not as much admired as they once were. Nonetheless, there are still many who see enough positive factors in Japanese management that those of us who wish to improve the system must work within this framework by preserving and strengthening the existing advantages even as we try to mitigate and eliminate the disadvantages.

Japanese Management and Japanese Economic Development

There is no question but that Japanese management has contributed significantly to Japan's industrial modernization and economic development. Yet it would be wrong to assume that Japanese management was the only factor, or even the main factor, in the successful modernization of Japanese industry around the turn of the century and Japan's spectacular economic growth after World War II. While it is true, as foreign scholars and analysts are fond of pointing out, that Japan turned itself into a modern industrial country with unprecedented speed, this was due to a number of other factors besides management.

The foundation for national unification had already been laid in the Edo period, and the Meiji government that came to power in 1868 vigorously promoted industrial modernization and better productivity. Private entrepreneurs also sought to develop new lines of business and to improve productivity. Both labor and management, while retaining their roots in the Japanese heritage, showed extraordinary enthusiasm for foreign culture, particularly for the production technology and lifestyles of the earlier-industrializing countries. The entire Japanese nation evidenced a strong desire for improvement in all aspects of industrialization, and a willingness to work hard to achieve it. The adoption of what is now known as Japanese management personnel policies was only one of a number of factors in Japan's successful rapid industrialization.

Once this basis was laid, the way was clear for rapid recovery after World War II within a favorable climate including the widespread introduction of automation and computerization, the Korean and Vietnam wars (with Japan serving as an important source of supplies but not involved in the fighting), and the government-business cooperation that has been referred to as "Japan, Inc.". In addition, Japan's postwar rapid economic growth was sustained not solely by large corporations but even more by the productive efforts of a myriad of small companies practicing only part of the Japanese management package.

Thus Japanese management was not the sole or even the primary force making Japan's industrial modernization and rapid economic development possible. Neither the wonder drug of the Japanese economy, nor is it a panacea for the economic ills which plague low-productivity societies.

Chapter 8

THE DISADVANTAGES OF JAPANESE MANAGEMENT

Four Disadvantages

Following the discussion of Japanese management's advantages in the previous chapter, this chapter will seek to examine some of the Japanese management's major disadvantages. Inherent in the system from the beginning, these drawbacks have become increasingly obvious in the postwar years. Among them, the four disadvantages that have had the greatest impact are:

1. Encouraging employee dependency and suppressing individual creativity

2. Discriminatory employment and impediments to the formation of a free horizontal labor market

3. Harmful effects of the escalator system and middle-management promotion gridlock

4. Work that gives no joy and seemingly has no meaning

These four disadvantages of Japanese management stem from factors present in the system's earliest forms. However, these factors did not come to be perceived as disadvantages until after World War II, and particularly in the late 1960s when Japan's economic growth slowed, the system's negative effects becoming increasingly apparent, and the high expectations fanned by the myth of Japanese management were disappointed.

The late 1960s were also the beginning of the golden age of automation — a time when automation and computerization became increasingly widespread in business and industry, evolving into such new fields as mechatronics and office automation. Due to the continuing recession, however, there was less expansion and less success in creating new workplaces, such that employees displaced by automation found themselves being laid off in personnel cutbacks or transferred to pre-automation waysides.

At the same time, the trend in industry was away from the traditional mass production of identical goods and toward smaller-lot production of more personalized and individualized products. Information-intensive industries moved into leading positions, and venture businesses created by corporate "dropouts" who wanted to give freer rein to their originality and inventiveness appeared in rapid succession.

There was renewed stress laid on originality and resourcefulness, and a new type of employee emerged more oriented toward independent thinking than toward traditional, groupistic diligence and less willing to patiently carry out simple, routine tasks. Among the young people hired in these new times, an increasing number were choosing a lifestyle conducive to self-expression and originality in which they could throw themselves whole-heartedly into work of their own choosing. Rather than opt for the traditional lifestyle of the average company man who spends his career in comfortable security under the giant company's wing, this new breed of worker chose to assume greater freedom with all of the responsibility that it entails.

In society at large, the aging of the population suddenly became a serious issue, and its effect was now felt within the company as the labor force became weighted toward the middle-aged and older employees.

As these trends progressed and changes in people's thought patterns became increasingly clear, the disadvantages of Japanese management, which had gone largely unnoticed in the past, gradually pushed their way into the public consciousness.

Encouraging Employee Dependency and Suppressing Individual Creativity

The first disadvantage of Japanese management, and that which has had the gravest lasting effect, is that it encourages employee dependency on the company while discouraging independence of spirit and any interest in self-expression or individual creativity.

Why does Japanese management have this negative effect? The primary factors that encourage dependency are the same practices that ensure employment stability, considered one of Japanese management's most appealing advantages. The uncomplaining Japanese employee can expect to enjoy the company's protection and benefits so long as he does a passable job, not rising above the average level and not distinguishing himself in any particular way, either good or bad. The company not only pays him a fixed salary each month but supplies him with all of the resources and facilities he needs for his work and in general looks after him in other various ways. The company also takes pains to see that the workplace is free of any conditions that might disrupt congenial worker relations, and the seniority-based hierarchy prevents contention and competition from developing among co-workers. All of these factors ensure a welcome employment stability, but they also foster an unhealthy psychological dependence on the company.

This dependence is a part of the *amae* psychology in which any group to which one belongs tends to be perceived as a close-knit community in which one is an integral part. When the group in question is a large firm or factory, the result is a pronounced tendency toward *amae* among employees.

Closely related to the encouragement of dependency, but more insidious in its effects, is the suppression of individual creativity and capabilities. Employees who feel strongly dependent on their company usually lack a willingness to deviate from its norms or risk incurring its displeasure. They lack the spirit of independence and have little inclination to display any individuality or creativity.

Dependent employees will naturally choose the secure life offered by a company career and seek to derive the maximum protection and benefits from the company. By contrast, an employee imbued with a strong urge to creativity will choose the opposite kind of life. While continuing his employment at the company, he will find his own goals in life outside of the company and pursue them as an independent individual giving full vent to his own capabilities. If the corporate bureaucracy will not allow him to do this, he will have the boldness to leave the company and start a venture business of his own with other like-minded individuals.

Why do most employees working within the restrictions of the Japanese management system lack this spirit and ability? There are at least two reasons. When the company hires employees, it evaluates them not according to their individual characteristics, originality, special capabilities, or personal ambitions but by their general character and educational credentials. If they are up to a certain level in these areas, they are hired as "whole people", not for any special qualities. The disregard of individuality and independence inherent in this traditional hiring policy is the first reason most employees lack initiative.

The second reason is the "grinder effect" of training employees in the standard skills the company needs, teaching them to respect the harmony of the workplace, and disciplining them to remove traits that differentiate them from their co-workers. Out of the raw material of new recruits is hewn a mass of average-capability salaried employees who excel in the social skills of harmony and accommodation but lack individuality, independence, and creativity.

The suppression of individual creativity affects not only general employees but also those in managerial positions. As is frequently pointed out, Japanese management turns out a large number of managers who are faithful to company policies and diligent in carrying out instructions but strikingly lacking in either the will or ability to innovate in leading the employees under them, improving work procedures, or developing new products. Even Ezra Vogel's *Japan as Number One,* while praising the benefits of Japanese management and arguing that there is much to be gained from transplanting Japanese management practices to America, warned that such a transplantation carries the danger of smothering employee individuality and creativity.[6]

Leona Esaki, who received the Nobel Prize for his invention of the Esaki diode, also pointed out in his recent book *America to Nihon* (The United States and Japan) that Japanese are generally less creative than Americans, and suggested that this was because the Japanese social climate was less conducive to creativity.[7] According to Esaki, the difference between the two peoples stems from the difference between the harshly competitive American social environment − an arena of open competition filled with people striving to exercise their individual abilities and creativity to win status with unique achievements − and the greenhouse-like Japanese social environment where harmony and congeniality are stressed in all situations − an environment that gives a person all the skills he needs in life and that extends a protective hand toward underachievers and people of lesser ability while ostracizing heretics and nonconformists. These two different environments produce two different types of people, one a nation of people with outstanding creativity and the other a nation of people who value going along over getting ahead.

This non-conduciveness to creativity, however, is not solely due to the two countries' different social environments. In Japan's case, there are also two particular social institutions that have contributed to the neglect of and even deliberate hobbling of creativity. One is the system of standardized school education, and the other is the personnel practices of large corporations operating under the Japanese management system.

The aim of Japanese school education, particularly since World War II, is to give all students standard, all-round training and turn out average "model pupils". Elitist channeling and differentiated education have been eliminated in the name of democratization. The curriculum during the nine years of compulsory education sadly lacks the kind of flexibility that might assist students in developing their individuality and creativity. There is no room for creativity, and the school environment is outwardly hostile to individuality.

Individuality and creativity have been further obstructed by the large corporations' policy of recruiting new graduates directly out of school at the end of the school year, and then subject them to standardized, uniform training. At the same time every year, these corporations administer entrance examinations for new graduates, evaluating and assessing these would-be employees not on their individuality, creativity, specialized capabilities, or personal ambitions but principally on their academic creden-

---

[6] Vogel, *Japan as Number One*: pp. 238-239.

[7] Leona Esaki, *America to Nihon* (Tokyo: Yomiuri Shinbun-sha, 1980).

tials and their general character, and those who meet these standards are hired en masse as total people. So long as the corporation follows this kind of recruitment policy, it cannot expect to acquire many employees overflowing with individuality and creativity or burning with the spirit of independence. Ever since the once-a-year hiring system was adopted after World War II, corporate officials administering the annual entrance examinations have complained that "this year's crop of applicants doesn't seem to have much spirit". What they fail to acknowledge, however, is that this spirit is largely discouraged precisely by their own basic recruitment policy.

This annual recruitment of new graduates is restricted to specific age groups. Should a person decide to attend a special educational or training facility to receive specialist training and to develop his individual talents or creativity, this will obviously add several years on to his education and thus put him over the big companies' hiring age limit – and if he tries to get the special education and make the age limit, he will more likely than not be missing several years of the standard education and thus find himself cut off for being sub-standard even though he might be above-standard in other ways. It is a no-win situation for the student, and few take the risk that such individuality entails. Parents who have sons and daughters approaching the start of their careers may want to send them off to specialist schools to develop their individual talents and creativity, but they almost invariably suppress this urge out of fear that it would ruin their children's chances on the corporate entrance examinations.

Once the new crop of recruits has been hired and the development of their resources has begun under the traditional Japanese management system, far from being encouraged to express their individuality or creativity, they are ground down until whatever creative spirit or special abilities they might have started with are smoothed out to a uniform level, leaving the corporation with a large number of congenial, cooperative, mediocre people of only average competence in the skills the company needs.

As a result of these recruiting and training policies, the typical Japanese businessman loses whatever individuality, creativity, and special skills he might have managed to retain despite the uniform, inflexible Japanese educational system. How can such people be expected to have any innovative will or ability in research and development, product development, market development, personnel development, and new planning? If the majority of Japanese businessmen continue to be cast in this mold, there is a very real danger that Japanese industry will soon be toppled from its position as "Number One", and it is imperative that the Japanese management system's recruitment and training policies be corrected as quickly as possible.

A number of executives have recently come to recognize the need to change these policies. Some of these people have taken it upon themselves to exhort the masses of new recruits to a greater sense of independence and more overt display of their individuality and creativity. This emerging recognition of at least one of the disadvantages of groupistic management practices is most encouraging, but all of these exhortations will be in vain if companies continue to preserve the traditional practices that encourage employee dependency and suppress individual creativity and abilities.

The specific practices of Japanese management that lead to the suppression of individuality are the regularly-scheduled, total-person recruitment system; training systems that turn out company men of only average ability; the rotation of personnel to produce flexible generalists; the discouragement of competition among employees and the stress on harmony; and the compassionate concern for the employee's total welfare extending even into his private life.

Discriminatory Employment and Impediments to the Formation of a Free Horizontal Labor Market

The second disadvantage of Japanese management arises mainly from its central practice of lifelong employment. This has two negative effects. The first is that it leads to discrimination against employees hired midway through their careers (still a relatively recent phenomenon), temporary employees, female employees, part-time employees, seasonal or day laborers, and other non-lifelong employees.

Large corporations generally recruit their regular employees from the large number of new graduates who apply each year and expect these people to stay with the company until they reach retirement. The corporation hires these new recruits en masse and takes them completely under its wing. Since the employees thus hired are seen as more important to the company than non-lifelong employees, they are given more thorough training, assigned to more important workplaces, given special treatment and consideration, and given more frequent opportunities for promotion. They are also the ones who receive the full benefits of the company's welfare facilities and services. In short, their status as lifelong employees entitles them to all sorts of special perks. If a person delays a few years after graduation before going to work for a large company, or if he spends a few years working for another company and thus brings prior career experience to his work, the company will usually not — unless it has specifically sought the individual out and hired him away from his other employer — afford him the same consideration and opportunities that it routinely grants people who came to the company directly from school. Still, employees who join in mid-career are often regarded as a type of regular employee, even if a suspect breed.

By contrast, temporary employees, part-time employees, day laborers, and other non-lifelong employees (including female employees) receive treatment and consideration a full rank below regular, lifelong employees. The large corporation regards its lifelong employees as its true constituency, and the rest are temporary help that the company would just as soon get along without if it could.

In the current labor shortage, women have come to be treated as an important part of the corporate work force, but until recently they were seen as inferior in status to the lifelong male employee. No matter how well qualified they may have been for their jobs, female employees usually quit work to become full-time housewives when they got married and had children. From the company's standpoint, it was only natural that the company should not want to invest as much in these "temporary" people and that they should be put on a different opportunity track from male employees of the same age, educational background, and years of service. Similar justification was found for the discrimination against temporary employees, day laborers, and part-time employees.

This type of discriminatory treatment, however, is now held to be unfair. There are, for instance, moves afoot to enact laws to prevent employment practices that discriminate against women. Arising from Japanese management's assumption that lifelong employment is a normal company practice, employment discrimination has today emerged as a major Japanese management disadvantage. Still, this particular disadvantage has been acknowledged at a relatively earlier stage than the other disadvantages, and efforts to correct it have also begun comparatively early.

A more far-reaching disadvantage of lifelong employment is that once an employee has taken a job with a large corporation, it becomes practically impossible for him to leave and join a different corporation. Lifelong employment was originally meant to promote employment stability and to enable employees at large corporations to work until retirement confident that minor failures or ineptitudes would not cost them their jobs. This system appeals, however, only if the employee is able to find work that suits him within the corporation and the corporation is willing to let him pursue it (and very few employees are so lucky), or if the employee is content to be an ordinary salaried worker satisfied with whatever work, rank, and treatment the corporation assigns him. For such employees, lifelong employment was and is extremely beneficial, and no doubt they would agree heartily with the saying that "a big tree gives the best shelter". But to a person who cannot satisfy his personal needs in the company, who suffers from the feeling that he has gotten into the wrong place by mistake, and who would like to find a company that offers more congenial work and change careers before it is too late, lifelong employment can seem more like life imprisonment — a cruel system whose motto is "Abandon all hope ye who enter here". While lifelong employment contributes to employment stability, it is a source of considerable unhappiness for some people.

Particularly in this age of increasing automation, when much work is turning into dull routine, a growing number of employees are dispirited at the prospect of spending a long time in the same company, rut and jump at the chance to leave and look for a company that is less mechanized. Lifelong employment, however, places major obstacles in the path of anyone who wants to move from one large corporation to another. The large corporations that have adopted the practices of Japanese management do not in principle forbid this labor mobility; in fact the Japanese Constitution guarantees the individual's freedom to choose his occupation. This is not always true in practice, however.

Because people hired as regular employees are expected to spend their entire careers at the same company, it is considered aberrant for a person to abandon one company for another. If a person is contemplating such deviant behavior, his peers and superiors alike will use various means to try to dissuade him. His immediate superiors in particular will feel responsible for this outbreak of deviance and will make the utmost effort to get the person to change his mind and not resign. If the person persists despite everyone's efforts to hold him back, he will be treated as something of a heretic, and his companions will turn their backs on him in the end. Most people abandon their job-hopping plans rather than endure such ostracism.

Unless a person is actively sought by the company he hopes to enter, the company is likely to resist hiring him in mid-career. Even if the person is eager to work and comes highly recommended, it is seen as contrary to the basic principle of lifelong employment to hire a person who has worked at another company. In particular, if there are rumors of disagreement between the person and his superiors in the company he is trying to leave, the company he is trying to join may well conclude that it would be wisest not to go out of its way to cause bad blood between the two firms. And if there was no attempt to stop the person from leaving, the company he wants to work for may conclude that his present company is letting him go so easily because he has no talents. In either case, it is not an easy switch — and once the person succeeds in moving from one large company where lifelong employment is practiced to another, his new employer will usually accord him much lower rank and treatment than would normally accompany the position he receives. Anyone wanting to move from one large company to another must be prepared to make this sacrifice.

Yet failure to change jobs has consequences far worse than the difficulties and disadvantages described above. The person who tries and fails to find another job with a large company faces either unemployment, an unimportant position in a small, unknown company, or continuation in his present company under a cloud of disgrace.

With all of the attendant difficulties and risks, it is no wonder that the number of people moving from one large company to another has been small. Thus, if all the large corporations in a given region preserve their lifelong employment policies, a free, horizontal labor market is unable to form in that region. A free, horizontal labor market is nothing if not the ability of laborers in a region to move freely among a large number of companies and to sell their services to new employers of their choosing.

Many of the large corporations have their own internal labor markets within which employees are rotated among different workplaces. This cannot, however, take the place of an external, free, horizontal labor market.

Harmful Effects of the Escalator System and Middle-management Promotion Gridlock

The third disadvantage of Japanese management is principally the result of another of its main practices: the seniority-based system of rewards. This system is often called an "escalator" system because of the way it works. The person who gets on first always stays ahead, and no one who gets on later can get in front of him.

The seniority-based hierarchy offers very real benefits to the employees of a large corporation. Even mediocre employees, as long as they obey orders and are patient, can expect to be promoted and be accorded better treatment almost automatically as they pile up more years of service with the company. This system has given untold numbers of less capable employees a feeling that their work was worthwhile. At the same time, because people are paid and promoted according to the objective standards of age and years of service rather than by their superiors' subjective evaluations of their work, it has served to reduce excessive competition and envy among employees of equal seniority in the workplace.

The disadvantage of this system is that it is, in principle, impossible for a person to be singled out for any special talents or accomplishments or to get ahead of anyone senior to him. Under the escalator system, even if an ambitious person applies his special talents to achieve major accomplishments, the corporation takes almost no direct notice of his feats, and certainly does not reward him with any special treatment. The person can only continue to wait together with his more mediocre colleagues until they all attain seniority and are given their scheduled promotions, nearly all at the same time. To the outstanding employee who knows that he has special talents and has achieved special results, the exaggerated impartiality of the company can only be a source of dissatisfaction. As time passes and this dissatisfaction festers, the employee loses the desire to do outstanding work or to contribute any more of himself to the company than he has to. The result is that the system creates a large number of outwardly efficient but inwardly mediocre and lazy company men who are "never idle, never late, but never actually working". This is detrimental not only to the employee with outstanding abilities but also to the company as a whole.

The seniority-based hierarchy has other drawbacks. The rising average age of the labor force, particularly noticeable in the years since Japan's rapid economic growth, is affecting the large corporation in that more and more people are staying healthy and continuing to work right up to retirement, such that a promotion gridlock has developed for employees under them in the hierarchy. Whereas the labor force's age demographics at large corporations had previously been pyramid-shaped with the largest number of employees at the 20–29 age group base, the upper 45–60 age group has gradually grown in number to give the pyramid a lumpier, more cylindrical shape. Although this swelling at the top of the pyramid is not yet as pronounced as in some industrialized Western countries, the labor force is aging four times as fast in Japan as, for example, in the United States.

This trend has brought the defects of the seniority-based hierarchy system into sharper focus. In the first place, it has created a jam at the top of the escalator. The lump at the top of the age structure includes the positions that carry the highest rank and most privileges, and now that these have been occupied, those just below them in line have to wait unjustly long to be promoted. This waiting can only hurt morale.

In the second place, the seniority-based salary schedule, which fit the old pyramid structure nicely, is now less acceptable with the new, top-heavy structure. With seniority-based wages and a pyramidal age structure, people in the upper age strata could and would normally be paid a higher salary than those in the lower age strata. With today's increasing number of older employees, however, corporations are finding it difficult to justify the total sum of these traditionally larger salaries. Since any company must be primarily concerned with whether or not its people are paying their way, this disadvantage in the escalator system is probably the one Japanese management feels most keenly.

Work that Gives no Joy and Seemingly Has no Meaning

The final disadvantage of Japanese management is the result of an unfortunate interaction between the system's authoritarian structure and the rapid automation of postwar years – these two factors combining to weaken employee identification with the company and erode employee morale.

It may seem contradictory, in the face of my earlier claim that

Japanese management fosters close employee identification with the company, for me to now claim the system takes the pleasure out of working and alienates employees from their companies. Yet there is no real contradiction because the direct causes of employee loyalty are the stable employment and flexible personnel practices of Japanese management, while the sense of futility and alienation stems from the fact that widespread automation has brought a halt to the democratic, participative practices originally present within the authoritarian Japanese management structure. Employee loyalty and employee alienation, while both originating in the Japanese management system, stem from different causes within that system. As a result, these two countervailing tendencies tend to work at cross-purposes within the large Japanese company, and it is the balance between them that determines how strongly Japanese employees do or do not identify with their company and their work.

The Automation Boom and Bureaucratization

Because Japanese management is founded in the groupistic belief that the continued prosperity of the company as a whole takes priority over the well-being of any one individual, this system is inherently authoritarian. Only a select few in the highest positions have the authority to speak for the corporation, and they use this position of authority to supervise everything done by people in lesser positions. Although such organizations are not authoritarian in the autocratic or totalitarian sense, they have an inherent tendency to develop into rigid, centralized bureaucracies. Given the right conditions, this can happen very easily.

One condition is that the organization be large, and a second is that it be extensively automated. These two conditions tend to arise in close association because it is common for corporate executives to try to make the organization more efficient by making it larger, subdividing the work more and more finely, and then automating operations.

When these two conditions coincide, Japanese management can easily lose the democratic, participative elements it originally contained and transform the organization into a rigid, centralized bureaucracy. The ease of this transformation comes from the intrinsic functional nature of automated systems. Automation makes work routine and concentrates control. As long as automation is kept small-scale and confined to individual departments at the lower levels of the organization, the equipment is run by rank-and-file employees. If the production activities of the employees in that department are already under small-group control, the automated equipment is likely to be programmed and run by the small group acting on its own initiative. In this case, the automation and routinization of work is confined to the individual workplace and employees have a sense of control over their work and its automation. Rigid, centralized bureaucratization does not occur in such cases.

Yet things are different when automation is introduced on a total scale so that it reaches into all departments and workplaces of a large organization. In this case, control of the system is centralized at the top of the organization and only the top people, or special operatives reporting directly to them, can start and operate the equipment following fixed, unchangeable programs created at the top. The other people in the organization — those at the middle levels and the large number of rank-and-file workers in the various workplaces at the bottom levels — have no say in deciding what equipment will be installed, when it will be installed, or what place it will have in what workplaces. Middle- and lower-level employees have no choice but to follow instructions and perform the same dull, standardized programs day after day. Automation raises productivity to unprecedented levels, but it also alienates employees from the results and poisons any pleasure they may have taken in their work.

Loss of Democratic, Participative Elements

Japanese management does not have to be a rigid, centralized industrial bureaucracy that alienates employees and deprives them of any joy or satisfaction with their work. Despite its authoritarian organization modeled on the close-knit communities of old, Japanese management in most cases allowed employees to take genuine pleasure in performing their given tasks. The reason why so many employees no longer have this satisfaction is that the democratic and participative elements of Japanese management have been rapidly eliminated in the years after World War II.

Japanese management originally included the bottom-up practices pointed out by Vogel, and *omikoshi* management first noted by Stanley S. Miller.[8] This bottom-up management refers to the practice of having the middle levels in the corporate organization — department sections, for example — plan new projects on their own initiative, obtain top management approval for it, and then carry it out on their own. *Omikoshi* management refers to the practice of having young employees in the rank and file of a company undertake group action on their own initiative so that they carry the company like a group of people carrying the small portable shrine (*omikoshi*) that is a traditional feature of Shinto festivals. Although they follow a predetermined route, they move along it in their own chosen way.

A system that gives people at the middle and lower levels of the organization the right to take management initiative this way is clearly

---

[8] Stanley S. Miller, "Management by *Omikoshi* — Traditional Features of Modern Business in Japan," in Paul L. Lawrence et al., *Organizational Behavior and Administration* (Homewood, Ill.: Richard Irwin, 1965): pp. 779-781.

democratized to an extent. A distinctive feature of this is that the people involved act not arbitrarily but in the spirit of participative management with regard to upper-level decision-making. Foreign analysts were quick to note these democratic, participative elements in the authoritarian Japanese management system. Harbison and Myers, for example, two of the original contributors to the myth of Japanese management, describe Japanese management as a unique mixture of highly centralized authoritarianism with democratic, participative management policies.[9]

Bottom-up decision-making and such forms of employee initiative as *omikoshi* management gave Japanese employees a certain creative leeway in deciding how to perform their assigned work. In many cases this made the work more enjoyable and made working more satisfying.

After World War II, however, when the technological revolution began to overtake Japan and the large corporations vied with each other in installing new electronic gadgets and automated equipment, the situation changed. The democratic, participative elements traditionally present in the authoritarian Japanese management system were rapidly swept away as the organization was automated. Part of the problem, of course, was the way Japanese corporations automated and computerized. Had the corporations started by introducing automation on a smaller scale — installing automated equipment only in a few departments or sections, for example, or adopting methods that would have encouraged bottom-up and self-management practices in newly automated workplaces —, had they not neglected to provide the necessary environment for the introduction of automation, there would not have been such a sudden loss of democratic and participative practices.

The Japanese tendency to rush to imitate everything done in other industrialized countries made many large corporations anxious to be the first to automate their entire organizations. The result was that authoritarian Japanese management lost its traditional democratic, participative elements and became a rigid, centralized, industrial bureaucracy. To the rank-and-file workers, this change represented a total rejection of individuality and creativity as, day after day, hour after hour, they were forced to repeat the same dull, uniform programs. Gradually the pleasure that they used to take in their work was eroded, and in its place there developed a feeling of alienation and worthlessness.

From Joy in Work to Delight in Leisure

Despite the effects of the automation boom, Japanese corporations still experienced rapid expansion through the mid-1960s and there was

---

[9] Harbison and Myers, *Management in the Industrial World:* p. 256.

plenty of new work for people to do. In the large firms that practiced Japanese management, the custom of rotating jobs meant that employees displaced by automation could be transferred to other workplaces where they were generally able to adjust quickly to new assignments. Even if the new industrial bureaucracy forced them to do simple, repetitive tasks, the personalized warmth of the Japanese management system and its many employee benefits usually buffered employees from the stark alienation felt by laborers in the industrialized countries of Europe and North America. As a result, large Japanese corporations tended to be optimistic that their employees would continue to identify strongly with the company and would continue to take pleasure and satisfaction in their work.

With the recession of the 1970s, however, the situation changed for the worse. Companies continued to enthusiastically embrace automation and computerization, but now the purpose was less often to raise productivity than to save on labor; in other words, to cut back on personnel while maintaining the same production levels as before. Employees displaced by these new labor-reduction policies frequently had no place to go, since the company was not expanding any more. The prospect ·of being laid off naturally soured any pleasure employees might have derived from their work and destroyed any sense that their fate and the company's were one. On the surface, they retained their traditionally high morale and close identification with the company, but was only a facade.

The highly touted QC (quality control) circle group activities started spontaneously at many large corporations in the late 1960s to rescue employees from the rigidity and restrictiveness of the industrial bureaucracy and to improve the quality of their work, which was then on the decline. In that most of these activities were informal and conducted outside the framework of regular production work, they do not represent any real attempt to reform the rigid industrial bureaucracy.

There have been many precedents for this phenomenon in the other industrialized countries: cases in which automation and computerization caused employee alienation and discontent resulting in lower morale and eroded will to work. Indeed, alienation and discontent tend to be stronger and more openly expressed in Europe and North America, and this alienation and lower morale are still semi-latent in the Japanese labor force. The fact that this alienation has yet to surface, however, does not mean that the industrial bureaucracy resulting from wholesale automation is any less restrictive in Japan than in the other industrialized countries. Rather, the lack of open discontent and hostility among Japanese workers is a tribute to the Japanese worker's adaptability as cultivated by the job rotation system and to the pacifying effect of employee benefits and personalized corporate concern for employee welfare.

It may also be that low employee morale is still only semi-latent in Japan because it is deeper-rooted than in other countries. By now, employees within fully automated industrial bureaucracies have probably already lost much of the joy and pride in their work that was once the foundation of their high morale. The resulting psychological vacuum is being filled by a 180-degree shift in value orientation as these people turn away from work and find their pleasure in leisure. If these employees continue to work hard at their jobs, it is usually so that they can enjoy their leisure better, and not for any sense of pleasure or pride in the work itself.

This loss of pleasure and pride in one's work also explains the widely-recognized phenomenon of general corporate stagnation, another very real negative effect that traditional Japanese management practices are having on the modern Japanese company.

Chapter 9

REFORMING JAPANESE MANAGEMENT

Rectifying the Disadvantages

Employees in major Japanese corporations have suffered immeasurable harm from the four disadvantages of Japanese management of (1) encouraging employee dependency and suppressing individual creativity, (2) discriminatory employment and impediments to the formation of a free horizontal labor market, (3) the harmful effects of the escalator system and middle management promotion gridlock, and (4) work that gives no joy and seemingly has no meaning. Although it is difficult to demonstrate this damage in tangible, specific form, it has clouded the lives of innumerable employees over the years.

Likewise, Japanese management as currently practiced has also had a crippling effect upon the corporation itself, although this impact is still semi-latent. Corporate executives are understandably slow to recognize the problems inherent in their own management system, but the negative aspects of Japanese management have been gradually paralyzing the corporation. Management tends to be more concerned with product development failures, misguided plant and equipment investments, productivity deterioration, or labor's wage demands, but the impact of unsuitable management practices is arguably even more insidious over the long term. The paralysis has become especially pronounced since the business recession of the 1970s. In the not-so-distant future, this could lead to lowered productivity, defective products or declining product quality, marketing difficulties, acrimonious labor relations, increased labor mobility, and recruitment difficulties.

While preserving the advantages of Japanese management, no time should be lost in rectifying its disadvantages. This is an urgent imperative for Japanese executives, management professors, and analysts and consultants. If we can eliminate the negative effects, we can at the same time reaffirm the advantages of Japanese management in a modern form and restore its international reputation.

It will be no easy task, however, to rectify the disadvantages of

Japanese management while preserving its advantages. In many cases the causes of the negative effects are closely intertwined with the causes of the positive effects. As has already been pointed out, for example, lifelong employment, while on the one hand leading to discriminatory employment practices and hindering the formation of a free, horizontal labor market, on the other hand provides the major benefit of employment stability. The same seniority system that creates middle-management promotion gridlock also underlies the company's flexible personnel policies and congenial atmosphere. Much the same could be said of the other practices of Japanese management.

If it were enough to remove the causes of the disadvantages, the solution might not be so difficult. Yet such a solution would also eliminate the most important, distinctive features of Japanese management and all of the advantages accruing from them. The task is therefore to modify and improve Japanese management practices so as to eliminate its negative effects while retaining its positive effects. This will be difficult and delicate work.

The reforms and modifications needed to solve this problem were the subject of an eighteen-month series of round-table seminars on Japanese management held recently with a dozen or so management professors and large corporation executives who share my concern about the future of Japanese management. While the results of these seminars are still incomplete and need further study on a number of points, it may be instructive to list them here as a possible starting point.

Restructuring Organizations

Eliminating the four main disadvantages of Japanese management requires first that the corporate organization be restructured and revitalized.[1]

1. The corporate organization should gradually be restructured at every branch and office. The existing rigid, centralized, bureaucracies should be dismantled and replaced by a more flexible, decentralized, and democratic organization of circles of authority. In both the central and outer circles, personnel should be divided into large numbers of small teams that conduct production- and information-related activities by autonomous decision-making and self-management processes. They should be flexible in the sense of being continually subject to both structural and functional reform, and they should work in close communication and cooperation with each other.

---

[1] Before carrying out any of the proposed organizational reforms that follow, the company must obtain the agreement of its labor union, because these organizational reforms are a type of labor participation in the management process. See Odaka, *Sangyo Shakaigaku Kogi*: Chapter IX, pp. 355ff.

2. The large number of workplaces in the outermost circle of the organization — where production actually takes place — should consist of autonomous teams of about a dozen skilled workers each. In addition to these production teams, each workplace should have teams of technicians and supervisors engaged in developmental and guidance work, free to move among the production teams, to give instruction in new, more efficient production technologies. Each production team, however, should be left to decide for itself what work methods to adopt and how to manage the work process and its results. Other production control circles could also be set up linking the outermost and innermost circles.

3. The innermost circle of the organization and the several offices situated immediately around it should consist of a number of autonomous teams. The innermost central circle should be filled principally with management and professional people assigned not to direct the activities of other workplaces or the organization as a whole but to facilitate the processing and exchange of information: analyzing reports sent in from the outer production sites, obtaining an overall picture of the entire firm or factory, and reporting the results back to the periphery. These people should also coordinate and approve proposals and provisional plans submitted by the peripheral workplaces via intermediate office channels and inform the periphery of these results. Clerical workers in the offices immediately surrounding the center are there to assist in this information processing and liaison work.

4. Overall policy plans — the basis for the central office's analyses and decisions — should be decided at general monthly meetings attended by everyone concerned. To improve the flow of information throughout the organization, the teams in each workplace within the central, intermediate, and peripheral circles should hold daily morning meetings presided over by their team leaders.[2]

5. Automation should not dominate the organization. Complete automation of the corporation will inevitably transform what was a democratic and dynamic organization into a rigid, centralized bureaucracy. Still some form of automation is necessary. Automation being such a certain source of higher productivity, rejecting automation completely would not be feasible even if it were possible. When automated equipment is installed, however, it should be installed only in those workplaces where it is appropriate, and should be entirely under the control of the workplace teams.

Meritocratic Personnel Policies

While these organizational reforms are being carried out, it will be

---

[2] A blueprint for this circular organization was given in Odaka, *Sangyo Shakaigaku Kogi:* Chapter IX, pp. 324-338.

necessary to begin reforming the specific practices that have sparked Japanese management's disadvantages. Personnel policies lead the list. As already seen, employee dependency and the suppression of individual creativity are caused by the practice of hiring people in large groups and bringing them en masse into company training programs that turn out average company men, job rotation to produce generalists, the suppression of competition and stress on harmony, and the corporation's all-embracing concern for the employee's personal well-being. The following general personnel policies would do much to reform and improve these practices and eliminate their negative effects.

6. Production personnel and candidates for executive positions should still be hired on a lifetime basis, but they should be selected not solely on the basis of their general character and academic record but with an emphasis on individual talents, skills, creativity, ambition, and other capabilities. (See also reform 22 below.) Applicants should be hired not only from each year's crop of new graduates but also from the larger pool of people with career experience.

7. Preference should still be given to hiring non-lifelong employees (temporary employees, part-time employees, outside help) as auxiliary production and office personnel, but they should also be hired on the basis of their individual talents, skills, and ambitions. (See reform 21 below.)

8. If employees originally hired as auxiliary personnel meet the necessary criteria, they should be upgraded to regular employee status.

9. In addition to the traditional training to produce generalists with all-round capabilities, both regular employees and auxiliary personnel should be given the intense, specialized training needed to develop particular skills, and the emphasis should gradually be shifted from generalist to specialist training. Job rotation should be confined to those employees who express a desire to become generalists.

10. After completing their training, both generalist and specialist candidates should be assigned as apprentices to teams in line with their desires, training results, potential, and temperament. After two or three years' experience, their achievements and capabilities should be carefully evaluated in placing them in new posts. This evaluation should be a regular event, and should take the individual's self-evaluations, qualification test scores, and other factors into consideration as well.

11. If an individual turns out to be unsuited to his post, he should be able, after a year or two, to apply for reassignment, take new qualifying tests, and be reassigned if he passes.

12. Should an employee perform exceptionally well at his assignment, he should be promoted, even if this means promoting him over the heads of other employees with as much or more seniority. If a young leader at one of the many production teams on the organization's periphery

does exceptionally well and is recognized by his peers and superiors as being capable of handling greater responsibility, for example, the central department should carefully evaluate his record and, if he is indeed qualified and wants the promotion, should immediately promote him to a position of greater authority, say assistant section manager, regardless of how old he is, how long he has been with the company, or how many other people might have more seniority. His salary, however, should not be conspicuously higher than what other people in his age group are paid.

13. With the agreement of the labor unions, the system of special promotions should be matched by a system of penalty demotions for employees guilty of gross negligence, violations of rules, laziness, and so on.

14. The system of special promotions and penalty demotions should be supported by the development of a stricter and more convincing system of monitoring the individual's performance.

15. In addition to special promotions, employees should also be promoted and given raises according to the traditional seniority-based system, but with the proviso that a person's performance both in his work to date and on qualification tests will be taken into consideration.

16. Executives should be divided into management and professional employees, the management people being generalists and the professionals specialists. Both groups should have about the same authority within the organization.

17. A person seeking to move into the management ranks should first have to complete his generalist education and training, be rotated among several jobs to acquire well-rounded experience, and serve as line foreman at one or more production sites. Anyone who does this and who has turned in above-average performances in his previous positions, has passed the appropriate examinations testing his managerial potential and his skills for the specific post he is seeking, and is recommended at all levels (by the people he worked for, the people he worked with, and the people who worked for him) should be considered management material. Age, seniority, and personal favoritism should not be factors.

18. A person seeking to become a professional specialist should first have to complete long and exacting specialist training, serve on the staff in several workplaces in his field of specialization, and serve as staff head in at least one of these locations. Fields of specialization might include production engineering, research and development, information processing, education and personnel, finance and accounting, and advertising. A professional candidate who has completed these requirements and satisfied conditions similar to those for management candidates should be treated the same as management candidates and given a position of equivalent authority.

Non-destructive Competition

Although it is a cause of employee dependency and a stifler of crea-tivity, the emphasis on harmony in the workplace should be retained. Yet over-emphasizing harmony can easily discourage healthy competition to the detriment of both the individual and the corporation. Harmony achieved only at the expense of motivation is harmony not worth having. Even in large corporations which purposely suppressed competition until recently, there was constant friction and competition just below the surface. What is needed is open and non-destructive competition to bring out the best in every employee.

19. The company should try to avoid measures that smother in-dividual talents and creativity and discourage employees from seeking personal distinction. Instead, employees should be allowed to create their own harmony through spirited competition. Harmony is not something that can be doled out by the company. This change of policy will doubtless disrupt much of the comfortably home-like atmosphere of the workplace, and might disturb employees who have become dependent upon the sheltered atmosphere. However, the need to compete in an open battle of ability and ingenuity will surely heighten the employee's individuality and creativity. This reform cannot, however, be implemented in isolation, and it will require the concurrent implementation of special promotions (reform 12), penalty demotions (reform 13), and performance-modulated seniority promotions (reform 15).

Less-intrusive Concern for the Employee

The traditional corporate concern for employee welfare, extending even into employees' personal lives, is probably the characteristic of Japanese management most responsible for encouraging dependence and *amae*. Corporate concern for employee welfare takes many forms as enumerated by Vogel in *Japan as Number One*: dormitories for singles and company housing for married employees, indoor and outdoor sports facilities, health facilities, hobby facilities, special family allowances, com-pany discounts on many of the everyday necessities, parties and other social events, lectures and other cultural activities, and so on. The list is nearly endless, and this extensive employee welfare network makes con-siderable demands on the company's time and money year after year. Unfortunately, the benefits of all this welfare are steadily decreasing while the detrimental effects come steadily to the fore. Most employees no longer regard these services in return for the lifetime of labor for long hours at low pay it exacts from them. Since World War II in particular, Japanese employees have become extremely cut-and-dry about these things, they do not feel either that the company is doing them any particular favor or that they owe it anything in return. Instead of tying the employee to the company in a positive way, these overprotective practices have the negative effect of dangerously encouraging employee *amae*. Drastic reform is in order.

20. These overprotective measures should be at least halved. The money saved could be used to raise employee salaries and bonuses, to improve occupational safety, to control pollution, or to provide better rest and recreation facilities. As an added benefit, excessive *amae* would be discouraged and the employee's self-reliance, independence, and creativity stimulated.

Eliminating Employment Discrimination and Encouraging a Horizontal Labor Market

The practice of lifelong employment is the primary culprit here. It is not necessary to eliminate lifelong employment completely, however, to eliminate its negative effects. The direct cause is not lifelong employment itself but the inflexible way it is applied. The large corporation usually recruits its production and executive personnel once a year, all about the same age and all from the year's crop of new graduates. These people are hired as lifelong employees and taken completely under the company's wing. The person is guaranteed a position in the company for life and the company provides him everything he needs to perform his work. In return, the recruit signs a contract entrusting essentially all his affairs to the company he enters. This practice is built on the lifelong employment system, but, because of it, large Japanese corporations treat anyone hired outside of this system, full-time employee and auxiliary personnel alike, as non-lifelong employees with less status.

Lifelong employment is also the main impediment to the creation of a free, horizontal labor market. Because of lifelong employment, Japanese companies expect the people they hire to stay with them until retirement, and they respond negatively to people who want to change careers and work for another company, and even to people wanting to sign up in mid-career. If someone wants to leave and go elsewhere, the corporation does not bother to ask why; it simply tries to stop him. If the person stubbornly insists that he wants to leave, he is frequently made a pariah. When the company he is hoping to join is also a large corporation practicing lifelong employment, it similarly assumes that employees will stay with the same company for life and may be reluctant to welcome anyone so obviously deviant as to want to change companies in mid-career. Even when the person manages to get in through the good offices of an intermediary, he will typically not have as much status as employees who have been with the company all their working lives. Little wonder that most people eventually abandon any job-hopping ideas they might have had. Quite a few employees find themselves in this fix, forced against their wills to remain permanently with their original firm like caged birds unable to escape, and the existence of large numbers of frustrated employees at Japan's big companies is prima facie evidence that the formation of a free horizontal labor market is being obstructed.

A number of reforms are necessary to correct this situation. Adoption of these reforms would, it is true, mean a substantial trimming of the traditional functions of lifelong employment, but that is one of the purposes of reforming Japanese management practices.

21. A greater proportion of the recruitment quota should be allotted to non-lifelong employees, and these non-lifelong employees should be given the same status and treatment as lifelong employees if their performance warrants.

22. Lifelong employees should continue to receive the same treatment and consideration as before, but they should not be treated so completely as "kept creatures of the company". With the agreement of the labor unions, the practice of guaranteeing employment for the person's entire working life should gradually be modified. Limits should be placed on the company's commitment to its employees. It should be possible for the company to fire even lifelong employees if they prove seriously incompetent, and the company should likewise be able to temporarily lay off substantial numbers of people in times of severe distress.

23. If a person with several years' experience expresses a desire to leave and go to work for another firm, if his reasons are good, and if the other company wants to hire him, then his present employer, rather than trying to dissuade him, should try to arrange for the change to take place under conditions advantageous to everyone concerned. Cooperation here would be much more appreciated than any of the cloying welfare benefits now offered.

24. The corporation should also grant early retirement and facilitate the search for post-retirement jobs for employees who want them. In addition to benefiting the individual, this would also help to relieve the current promotion gridlock that is frustrating so many middle-management employees.

Redesigning the Escalator

As noted earlier, this promotion gridlock is largely rooted in Japanese companies' escalator-like seniority system. Many of the reforms suggested above will also have a beneficial effect here, yet they should be supplemented by one more reform specifically directed at reforming the seniority escalator:

25. In all workplaces, job assignments should be redesigned or created for older employees, and personnel should be reassigned to relieve the promotion jam at the upper age levels.

Restoring Employee Pride in Work

The unfortunate combination of Japanese management's authoritarian organization and the large-scale automation that was introduced after World War II has left many employees feeling that their work is neither enjoyable nor worthwhile. Extensive and all-encompassing automation has swept away the democratic, participative elements traditionally present in the organizational structure, vitiating any pride and pleasure which people might derive from their work.

The first step needed to remedy this is to restore Japanese management's democratic and participative elements. The second step is to revise the way companies automate. Both of these steps have been outlined more specifically in the first five reforms, specifically the suggestion that the organization be democratized with the creation of a large number of circles of small, autonomous teams in the peripheral workplaces and the suggestion that automation be done in specific workplaces and not dominate the company.

Other approaches include:

26. The organizational framework within which automation is adopted should be gradually changed from a rigid, authoritative, pyramidal structure to a more decentralized and flexible structure composed of small, autonomous teams.

27. Regular employees who want to take qualification tests for assignment or reassignment to one of these smalll autonomous teams for a fixed period of time should be allowed to do so.

28. The teams should have the functional flexibility needed to adapt to changes in company policy or the general business climate. Likewise, the teams' makeup and operational methods should also be flexible. All changes, however, should only be made in consultation with all employees in the workplaces involved.

29. The small, autonomous teams should be self-managed. Working hours should be adjusted as appropriate, or team members placed on flex-time schedules and free to set their own hours. Before this change can be made, however, each workplace's work schedule for a given period should be decided upon in consultation with all employees concerned.

30. Effective teamwork and self-management will require skills and experience over and above what is needed with the traditional workplace organization. Organizational reform alone is unlikely to boost employee morale unless people are given the necessary skills and experience to cope

with their new situation. Team leaders and supervisors should therefore be trained in the methods of acclimating team members to the new system and teaching them the skills they need.

Chapter 10

IS JAPANESE MANAGEMENT TRANSPLANTABLE?

So far, I have discussed the differences between the reality and the myth of Japanese management; the origins of Japanese management; the group-centered value orientation that guided its formation; the advantages and disadvantages that it has had for Japanese companies and employees; and the reforms needed to eliminate its current disadvantages. One last question remains: the question of whether or not Japanese management practices can be successfully transplanted overseas, as the myth naturally assumes they can – specifically whether or not Japanese management would yield the benefits hoped for if transplanted to a modern, advanced industrial country such as the United States.

With the negative effects of Japanese-style management beginning to outweigh its positive effects even within Japan, it is extremely doubtful that Japanese-style management will have the mythical benefits attributed to it if it is transplanted overseas in its present form. Yet now that Japanese management's disadvantages have been acknowledged and reforms proposed for their amelioration, if Japanese management is reformed along the lines proposed and its disadvantages rectified to develop a new set of Japanese management practices more closely approximating the myth, it should be possible to effectively transplant the new and reformed system of Japanese management to other industrial countries.

However, this seemingly simplistic answer needs some clarification. Assuming the suggested reforms are made, it is quite likely that reformed Japanese management could be transplanted relatively easily to some types of countries and could function effectively in their industrial environments, but it is also likely that transplantation would be more difficult to other regions and that the anticipated benefits might not be forthcoming even if the transplant were effected. It is only natural for the Japanese, as the creators and reformers of the Japanese-style management practices, to believe that their system has a universal validity and will function effectively wherever it is adopted. Yet other countries' value sets and social customs differ sharply from those in Japan, such that anyone attempting to transplant and use Japanese management abroad must be prepared to encounter many obstacles. As mentioned earlier, even Ezra Vogel's *Japan as Number One: Lessons for America* warned that serious problems are likely to be encountered in trying to transplant Japanese management to the very different American context.

Certainly it should be possible for corporate executives in particular countries to extract those features of Japanese management they admire — lifelong employment and *omikoshi* management, for example — and to introduce them into their own industrial systems to good effects. Yet this is not Japanese management. Japanese management is a tightly integrated system of five or more separate-yet-intertwined practices functioning together, and transplanting Japanese management has to mean transplanting the whole system if it means anything. Such a transplant would undoubtedly encounter obstacles and trigger unexpected consequences in a country such as the United States.

The question is where the attempt to transplant Japanese management might be successful and where it would be difficult and perhaps harmful. The fact that different countries and regions exhibit a wide range of social customs and value sets, are at different stages of development in different industries, and have very different labor situations argues against any attempt to place specific countries or regions in one category or the other. Much study still needs to be done to determine which combinations of factors make a given country or region receptive to Japanese management. Accordingly, the following criteria should be understood as a purely provisional effort to suggest some of the considerations involved.

1. In general, it should be easy to transplant Japanese management practices to countries such as those of Southeast Asia where there is a social tradition of groups formed on the principles of groupism or analogous principles and where society is characterized by interpersonal cooperation, harmony, and loyalty to the group. This is true regardless of the present stage of industrial development, and transplanting the reformed Japanese management system should yield the expected benefits for industry in these countries.

2. For Western European countries and the United States, where organizations tend to be founded on the values of individualism rather than groupism, competition rather than harmony, and where organizations generally stress productive efficiency and devotion to the purposes of the organization as measured by the results achieved rather than the effort made, it will probably be very difficult to transplant even the reformed Japanese management system, and the attempt would likely be counterproductive in a number of ways. This does not, however, mean that it is impossible to transplant Japanese management to such countries. It simply

means that special efforts and special measures will be needed to dismantle the barriers, eliminate the harmful effects, and make the transplant feasible.

3. Japanese firms with overseas business operations in either type of country should abandon the traditional system of Japanese management and adopt the reformed version in its place. Otherwise, they are unlikely to derive any benefits at all from using Japanese personnel policies overseas.